What people are saying about *Help! They Want Me to Fundraise!*...

Get this book! If the only *thing you read is "CEO Fundraising Knowledge and Community Connectedness" in Chapter Two, your return on investment will be* immeasurable. *But don't stop there. Susan Black does a masterful job of dismantling myths about fundraising and replacing them with insightful realities, inspiring readers to redirect their charitable organizations into vastly brighter futures.*

M. Kent Stroman, CFRE
Author, Speaker, Consultant

Susan Black has created a clear, readable text to guide nonprofits through the relationship building and planning required for successful fundraising. Nonprofits of all sizes will benefit from this book, and I encourage board members and professional or volunteer staff to read and complete the activities together to build capacity and increase effectiveness. Bravo, Susan!

Kerri Laubenthal Mollard, MA
Founder and Principal Mollard Consulting LLC

This book is just what the fundraising field needs! If you are new to fundraising, **Help! They Want Me to Fundraise!** *should be your go-to manual. Susan Black has broken down the fundamentals of fundraising in such a way that the reader will have the tools required for success. A must-read for all staff and volunteers new to fundraising.*

Lisa S. Courtice, PhD
Executive Vice President, The Columbus Foundation

This book is a terrific fundraising primer! It should be required reading for all reluctant or inexperienced nonprofit trustees who discover they must fundraise to fulfill their fiduciary duties. Every nonprofit executive of a charitable organization should make this a centerpiece for board orientation.

Dean Pulliam, MS, CAE
Executive Director, Autism Society of Ohio

This book would have saved me years of trial and error at the beginning of my fundraising career! It is the best step-by-step guide to fundraising I've encountered.

Shaunacy Webster
Founder and President, Webster Communications Group

Susan Black takes the seemingly overwhelming task of fundraising and breaks it down into manageable tasks. In short, she shows readers how to eat the fundraising elephant one bite at a time. This is the perfect guide for new development directors, volunteer development committees, and chief executives struggling to add fundraising to their "to-do" lists. With its worksheets, resources, and real-world examples, **Help! They Want Me to Fundraise!** *is a must-have for any new fundraiser's library.*

Susannah E. Shumate, MA, CFRE
Principal, Work of the Heart Consulting

Susan Black provides a practical, actionable approach to fundraising that can be applied to any nonprofit organization regardless of mission. As a volunteer turned full-time staff member of a nonprofit, I keep this book within arm's reach, and it will remain one of my staple resources.

Aimee R. Dearsley
Business Manager, Stray Rescue of St. Louis

This book is a gem! Readable, inspiring, and filled with the basic info we all need to engage in successful fundraising. Susan Black's engaging style keeps you turning pages. At the end, you'll feel both prepared and inspired to use your passion to build fundraising relationships!

Rev. Steve Putka
President of the Board of Directors
United Methodist Community Ministries of the Capital Area District

If fundraising can be characterized as picking pockets for the public good, then Susan Black is Fagin and this book is a back alley in nineteenth-century London. When you have the chance, m'dears, it's always wise to learn from the best.

Ken Keller
Author, Communications Professional, Community Volunteer

Susan Black has applied her extensive knowledge and skill into a useful and entertaining book. Any executive director who purchases **Help! They Want Me to Fundraise!** *will be equipped with an effective tool to initiate a fundraising program with staff and board.*

Fran K. Wesseling
Executive Director, Foundation For the Challenged

Help! They Want Me to Fundraise!

A Nonprofit Fundraising Manual for Beginners

Susan Black, MA, CFRE

Help! They Want Me to Fundraise! A Nonprofit Fundraising Manual for Beginners

One of the **In the Trenches™** series

Published by
CharityChannel Press, an imprint of CharityChannel LLC
30021 Tomas, Suite 300
Rancho Santa Margarita, CA 92688-2128 USA

CharityChannel.com

ISBN Print Book: 978-1-938077-47-0 | ISBN eBook: 978-1-938077-48-7

Library of Congress Control Number: 2013952109

13 12 11 10 9 8 7 6 5 4 3 2 1

Printed in the United States of America

This and most CharityChannel Press books are available at special quantity discounts for bulk purchases for sales promotions, premiums, fundraising, or educational use. For information, contact CharityChannel Press, 30021 Tomas, Suite 300, Rancho Santa Margarita, CA 92688-2128 USA. +1 949-589-5938

Publisher's Acknowledgments

This book was produced by a team dedicated to excellence; please send your feedback to editors@charitychannel.com.

We first wish to acknowledge the tens of thousands of peers who call charitychannel.com their online professional home. Your enthusiastic support for the **In the Trenches™** series is the wind in our sails.

Members of the team who produced this book include:

Editors

Acquisitions Editor: Linda Lysakowski

Comprehensive Editor: Stephen Nill

Copy Editor: Jill McLain

Production

In the Trenches Series Design: Deborah Perdue

Layout Editor: Jill McLain

Administrative

CharityChannel LLC: Stephen Nill, CEO

Marketing and Public Relations: John Millen

About the Author

Susan Black, MA, CFRE, is the owner and principal consultant of Allene Professional Fundraising in Columbus, Ohio. *Help! They Want Me to Fundraise!* is her first book. As a fundraising consultant, Susan prides herself on utilizing proven fundraising techniques to provide a personalized approach to the fundraising needs of all kinds of nonprofit organizations.

After earning a bachelor's degree and a master's degree in political science from Mary Baldwin College (Staunton, Virginia) and the University of Richmond (Virginia), respectively, Susan began her career in development as a prospect researcher at Marietta College (Marietta, Ohio). She gained additional experience as a development director at Easter Seals of Central and Southeast Ohio and the Epilepsy Foundation of Central Ohio before serving as vice president of advancement for five years at St. Vincent Family Centers in Columbus, Ohio.

Susan founded Allene Professional Fundraising in 2008 to bring her expertise to the wider nonprofit community and help struggling nonprofits identify strategies that will allow them to reach their potential. She is an active member of the Association of Fundraising Professionals and the Kiwanis Club of Columbus. She first received her Certified Fund Raising Executive designation in 2006 and was recertified in 2009 and 2012.

Susan can be reached through her website at allenefundraising.com.

Dedication

This book would not have been possible without my greatest blessing, my husband John, whose support and sacrifices make owning my own business a reality. I dedicate this book to him.

Author's Acknowledgments

There are two colleagues and friends who brought this book to fruition. Fran Wesseling, executive director of Foundation For the Challenged, was the driving force behind the original manuscript of the book. That manuscript was made available to her constituents and formed the major part of the book. Shannon Carter, dear friend and colleague, completed much of the research and formatting of the original manuscript. Her care and support made writing the book many times easier than it would have been otherwise. I'd also like to acknowledge Stephen Nill and Linda Lysakowski of CharityChannel Press, who were so supportive, helpful, and encouraging to me as a first-time author. Many thanks to all these incredible people for helping me achieve this milestone.

Contents

Summary of Chapters

Chapter One

What Is Fundraising, and Why Is It Important? Chapter One helps readers understand how "those organizations" that seem to have all the money and press coverage are doing it. An assessment of fundraising is provided in this chapter as well as a review of how important it is to get started today because of the new economy.

Chapter Two

The First of the Four Building Blocks of Fundraising Success. Chapter Two gets into the meat and potatoes of the book by introducing the first building block, organizational readiness. Building on the information provided in the first chapter, this chapter covers the main components of organizational readiness: financial stability, board capacity/preparedness, CEO fundraising knowledge and community connectedness, development staff preparedness, and backroom operations.

Chapter Three

Building Block Two: Fundraising Goals and Plans. Chapter Three explains the importance of having a strategic plan and a fundraising plan that work in tandem. It also explains the components of a case for support and why having a case is critical to sharing the mission and vision of the organization with potential donors.

Chapter Four

Building Block Three: Primary Fundraising Vehicles. Chapter Four provides an overview of the various vehicles for fundraising. The explanations are provided for those reading the book who are not familiar with these vehicles or who have heard of them but are not familiar with how they work. Specific advice and/or step-by-step guides for developing or implementing these vehicles are provided.

Chapter Five

Building Block Four: Communications and Community Relations. Chapter Five covers the last of the building blocks, communications and community relations. Emphasis is placed on crafting a story and telling it as well as creating ongoing communication vehicles for communicating the story to donors.

Chapter Six

The CEO as Chief Fundraiser. Chapter Six is dedicated to those who have recently been assigned the job of fundraising, need to start a program from scratch, or are CEOs without fundraising staff. The chapter includes encouragement and advice about how to get started and the keys to being successful in fundraising as the CEO.

Chapter Seven

What to Do If It's Just You. If you are the only person working in the area of fundraising in your organization and are new to the role, this is a quick-start guide to setting up shop.

Chapter Eight

Avoiding Common Pitfalls in Your Fundraising Career. As you begin a fundraising career, whether as an executive director, a development director, a board chair, or a volunteer, consider the potential pitfalls mentioned in this chapter and plan ahead to avoid them.

Appendix A

A Fundraising Readiness Assessment. A great place to start or finish this manual by assessing your readiness for fundraising.

Appendix B

Fundraising Training Resources. A list of great resources to help you, your CEO, or your board find more fundraising training.

Foreword

Where do I even begin to thank my dear friend and colleague, Susan Black, for giving what I believe to be one of the greatest educational gifts to our profession, especially to those who are being asked to fundraise and have no idea where to begin?

I love to read, and after twenty-seven years of consulting, I have read hundreds of books on various fundraising topics, such as strategic plans, development assessments, capital campaigns, planned giving, and many others. But this is the first book I've read that gives novice fundraisers the key information they need to get started quickly and efficiently. I call Susan's book a gift because that is exactly what it will be to the hundreds, if not thousands, of people searching for a comprehensive, "how-to-get-started" fundraising manual who have been unable to find one. Susan has come to the rescue! She masterfully takes what can be viewed as an overwhelming task and boils it down into a very succinct and manageable process.

I think of Susan's book as a GPS for fundraising, because she doesn't just show you the process—she walks and talks you through it with powerful personal stories and best practices, all while weaving compassion and words of encouragement into the directions. In the beginning of Susan's book, she talks about the number-one trait she believes you need to have to be a successful fundraiser: passion. You will very quickly feel Susan's passion for fundraising and teaching as you read the worksheets, assessments, and resources she has prepared. She encourages you to answer specific questions about solicitation methods, prospective funders, donor communications, and many other key fundraising processes. By posing challenging questions, Susan forces you to stop, give some thought, dig deep, and be completely honest. By going through this process, you will end up with valuable information that you will use to then develop specific plans for your fundraising program.

Susan's book is also a gift to me and other fundraising consultants who receive inquiries from those who are getting started in fundraising. Many times when I meet with these organizations, I find that their basic knowledge of fundraising is so limited that it is challenging to discuss specific development strategies. I will now recommend they read *Help! They Want Me to Fundraise!* to provide a comprehensive overview of fundraising. I know that because of the valuable advice and counsel Susan provides, readers will see the big picture of how a fundraising program comes together, the steps to be taken, the pitfalls to avoid, and how "those organizations," as Susan so humorously refers to them, get all that money and press! I sincerely believe it will become an invaluable resource manual for development officers throughout their careers, whether they are launching a new program or considering a capital campaign.

Finally, Susan's book is a gift to the fundraising profession. As a smart and strategic fundraiser, Susan could have chosen to write a book focused on a new and trendy topic. Instead, she decided to step back, and give back, by sharing valuable lessons to make the road less bumpy for those new to fundraising. I appreciate this because it shows Susan's caring heart for those new development professionals working in small shops or those who may need to build a development program from the ground up.

So if you are new to fundraising or find yourself in need of a great, easy-to-read guide to fundraising basics, then give yourself a wonderful gift and keep reading! Then, when you're finished, I recommend that you do what I plan to do: buy several copies, wrap them up with a big bow, and give this gift to other people you know who need help launching a fundraising program. It's definitely the gift that keeps on giving!

Michelle Cramer, CFRE
President and CEO
Cramer & Associates Inc.

Introduction

If you have this book in your hands, it's likely that you are a person in need of a plan. Perhaps a nonprofit organization you care about needs to raise money. You may serve as a volunteer or board member for this organization, or you may be employed as its executive director or new development director. It's even possible that in the past you worked with another organization that raised money—maybe even a lot of money—but you weren't the one in charge. Now someone has asked you to step up to the plate, and you're not even sure what this is going to require or if your organization is ready.

I bet you could use a little good news, so here it is: you have found the book you need to get started. That's the first bit of encouragement I have for you. The second is this: you can do this!

You may be thinking: "How can anyone expect me to do this?" Believe me, I have seen all kinds of people who are fundraisers: introverts and extroverts, technical people and artistic people, right brained and left brained. While your personality and your experience will have some impact on your ability to raise money, according to the Association of Fundraising Professionals, the following things are the most important characteristics of fundraisers:

- Passion
- Reliability/follow-through
- Ethics and integrity
- Ability to listen well
- Ability to tell a story
- Strong values and a desire to make a difference
- Dedication to and belief in the cause

> One of my former bosses loved to tell the story of why she hired me for my job. Believe it or not, it's because I cried in my interview! I didn't mean to, honestly! I don't remember what her question was, but I do remember I said something to the effect of, "In my career, I've worked mostly with disability organizations. You think you've seen the worst you can see, and then you see something even worse." I started to tear up thinking about the people I had met and the families I had interacted with, and before I knew it, I was getting emotional. My former boss said she knew at that moment that I was extremely passionate about the causes I served, and that characteristic was exactly what she was looking for. I don't recommend crying in your interview, but in my case, I got the job!

Notice that the first thing on the list is passion. I would say that other than being reliable and ethical, passion is the only characteristic that can't be learned or gained along the way. If you aren't passionate about your organization or your cause, you will not be an effective fundraiser. But since you are passionate, I want you to know that you can do this. You already possess the most important thing.

Since you possess the most important characteristic, everything else can be learned. There is both an art and a science to fundraising. You can learn the science and you can develop the art. You don't need to know everything at the beginning, just some key things that if applied, practiced, and developed can lead your organization to fundraising success. That's what this book will provide you.

Now you still may be thinking, "That's nice, but you don't know my organization. It's a mess." Many times in my career, I've been in the seat where you're sitting, tasked with raising money for an organization that has a limited track record in fundraising, has few relationships with individual donors, and is virtually unknown in the community. I've also worked for organizations whose leadership was falling apart or altogether absent, that had some form of stigma surrounding their mission or clients, or that had boards that stubbornly refused to participate in fundraising. In the words of Dr. Martin Luther King Jr., my career has been about "making something out of nothing, and a way out of no way." I am proud to say I have done everything in my career from run a bingo game to raise a million dollars.

This is the experience I bring to you throughout this manual. It is a quick-start, how-to guide to help organizations with novice fundraising staff or volunteers assess their readiness for fundraising and develop a basic plan for getting started. By the time you have finished the manual, you will:

- discover the key ingredients that are necessary to be successful at fundraising;
- assess which of these keys to fundraising success your organization possesses or lacks;
- identify what you can do to address your deficits and build on your strengths; and
- create a road map for future fundraising success.

You will find that I am brutally honest in my advice. There are no magic beans, no silver bullets, no money trees, and no "get rich quick" schemes. But there are techniques and skills that can be gained. You can put the concepts, suggestions, and action steps in this book into practice and build a fundraising program from nothing. And with personal experience, you will add art to this science as well. Ultimately, with perseverance and good luck, you can build a legacy of sustainability for your organization.

I have done it and so can you.

Chapter One

What Is Fundraising, and Why Is it Important?

IN THIS CHAPTER

- Understand the basic definition of fundraising and uncover the secret ingredient
- Learn the industry standards for professional fundraising
- Explore the donor pyramid
- Get a crash course in the new economy

In this chapter, you'll learn what professional fundraisers know about fundraising techniques and practices, and you'll have an opportunity to assess your current fundraising activities. You'll also learn why fundraising is so important in the new economy and why you need to prepare your organization for it.

A Basic Definition of Fundraising

I work with boards of trustees frequently. Most board members know that a part of their job is fundraising. Unfortunately, most board members equate fundraising with a root canal. Why? I believe it's because most people are afraid of fundraising due to the mistaken idea that fundraising means begging for money from people who don't want to give it.

While asking people for money is critical to fundraising, there is only one universal law of fundraising, and that is that it's all about relationships, relationships, relationships. As fundraisers, we invite people to have a relationship with our organizations, and through these relationships, we ultimately change the world.

A Tale of Two Missionaries

Over the years, I have heard many missionaries speak at my church. One time a young missionary came to our church and did a special presentation. At the end, he awkwardly asked for support, apologizing for the request and downplaying his needs. I don't know what kind of offering the missionary received that day, but I have never seen him again. Contrast this with another young missionary who made a presentation about the difference his work was making in his mission field, shared testimonies of the lives changed, confidently stated his financial need, and asked for both our prayers and our monetary support. The difference? He returns yearly to our church and receives much of his annual support from our congregation. The moral of the story is this: *never* apologize for asking for financial support for a cause about which you are passionate.

That is fundraising. Do we have to ask people for money? Yes, but not only in a transactional way (like paying for a ticket). As a professional fundraiser, I am part of a noble profession that connects people's passions with the right philanthropic missions. For me, this is the most incredible job in the world.

In order to be successful in fundraising, you and your organization's leadership need to see fundraising as a means to create lasting relationships that will sustain your organization long term. Let's look at how you can begin building these relationships for your organization and why it's so important.

Components of Professional Fundraising and the Fundraising Pyramid

You've probably wondered about "those organizations" in your community that seem to get all the support and positive PR. "How do they do it?" you think, as you toil away to raise even the most modest dollar goals. Let's take a look.

How "Those Organizations" Do It

"Those organizations" differ from yours in that they are conducting their fundraising using industry standards and best practices. In other words, they are conducting their fundraising in a professional manner and investing the necessary dollars to make that possible. Your organization is doing some of the same things those other organizations are doing, whether you realize it or not. Do you have an annual event? Do you send out solicitation mailings even if it's just an envelope in your newsletter? Submit grant proposals? Ask board members to solicit their companies? Have a website with a "Give Here" button? Then you are utilizing standard methods of fundraising too.

Most large nonprofit organizations utilize similar methods for raising dollars. They raise them from individuals on an annual basis (annual giving) for special program purposes (special giving or major gifts) or for capital needs (capital campaigns). They raise them from corporations and private foundations (corporate and foundation relations). And they raise them from bequests given through wills and estates (planned giving). Some raise them through earned income (fees for service or retail operations) and some as social entrepreneurs (mission-driven businesses that raise dollars for reinvestment into the charitable organization).

Your Fundraising Vocabulary

Annual giving: Any gift given by an individual or business on an annual basis and/or through events, mail solicitations, telemarketing, or radio or TV (i.e., "radio-a-thons" or telethons).

Special giving: Usually a one-time gift given for a specific purpose or program need.

Major giving: Gifts given from assets of an individual donor, over time, for a specific purpose.

Capital campaigns/capital giving: Gifts and pledges made toward brick-and-mortar projects and/or equipment.

Corporate and foundation giving: Direct cash gifts from corporations for general operating support; grants from corporations, corporate foundations, and private foundations for a specific programmatic purpose. Government grants may also fall in this category.

Planned giving: Gifts given through estate plans, wills, life insurance, and trusts.

Earned income: Income earned from a service or sales of a product that is used for operating revenue. Examples include thrift stores, restaurants, and janitorial services.

Social entrepreneurs: A description of organizations that create earned income from the operation of mission-driven businesses. These organizations raise dollars for reinvestment into the charitable purposes of the organization and simultaneously achieve social change.

definition

Remember when we talked about the importance of relationships in fundraising? Well, another way to think about these common fundraising techniques is by considering how people begin their relationship with an organization. One of the best ways to illustrate this idea is by using the time-honored donor pyramid.

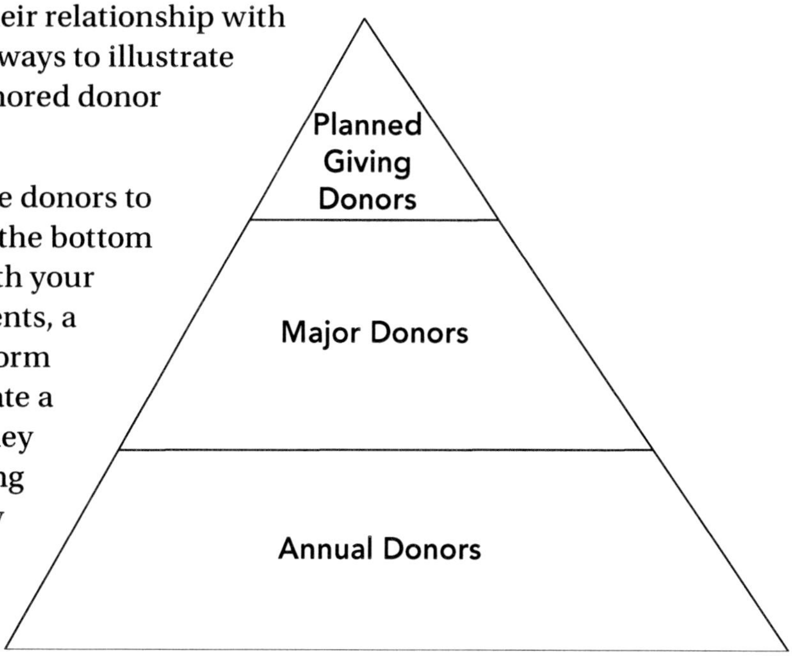

Planned Giving Donors
Major Donors
Annual Donors

Out of the universe of prospective donors to your organization, most donors (the bottom third) will have a first contact with your organization through special events, a mail solicitation, or some other form of "annual giving." As you cultivate a relationship with your donors, they "move up the pyramid," becoming consistent donors and eventually becoming interested in making major gifts or planned gifts. While it's possible to receive a major gift or planned gift without first receiving an annual gift from a donor, it's less typical than the route just described.

These descriptions of standard industry practices should give you a working knowledge of how most large organizations raise funds. To help you actualize these ideas, let's take a quick look at what you are doing currently in the way of fundraising.

On the worksheet below, *Current Fundraising Activities Assessment*, simply indicate "yes" or "no" to each item and list any other fundraising vehicles you currently have that are not listed. Leave the final column on the right blank for now and we'll address that momentarily.

Current Fundraising Activities Assessment

Item	Yes or No	Type of Giving
Envelope in newsletter		
Annual solicitation letter		
"Give Here" button on website		
Host an event		
Submit grant proposals		
Board members request gifts from their employers		
Participate in United Way campaigns or other types of workplace giving campaigns (combined federal campaign, combined charitable campaign, combined health campaign, etc.)		
Other type here:		
Other type here:		
Other type here:		

Now consider each of your existing fundraising techniques and ask yourself what type of giving this method represents. For instance, your "Give Here" button is most likely to solicit an annual gift from a donor, while your grant request solicits a major gift. Holding a special event is an annual giving activity. Go ahead and indicate the type of giving each fundraising activity represents now.

Do you notice anything? I'll bet that most of your activities solicit annual gifts and that very few, if any, solicit major or planned gifts. While we'll dig deeper into these subjects later in the manual, here's the "take away" from this exercise for now.

- You probably have some things you are already doing that are considered standard fundraising practices. Good for you!

- Most of those are likely to be annual giving activities that solicit smaller, ongoing gifts from new or repeat donors. That's good because it means you are establishing and then building relationships with individual donors.

- It's unlikely you have anything in place to solicit major or planned gifts other than grant requests. That's okay, but it also indicates a need for further donor cultivation.

- Cultivating donors so they entrust you with larger gifts will require new tactics and techniques you may not currently possess, but—and here's the important thing—having major donor prospects is the difference between organizations that succeed long term at fundraising and those that don't.

For those readers who answered "no" to everything and therefore didn't complete the right column, never fear. Just remember that these are great starting points to consider as you make your fundraising plans.

Why Fundraising Is Important to Your Organization

Now you know that relationships are the secret ingredient to successful fundraising and that using industry standards can help strengthen relationships, but you may still be skeptical about your organization's ability to undertake fundraising. You may also have board members who don't see the need, primarily because they don't want to do it. So before we go on to learn more about preparing your organization for successful fundraising, let's talk about the new economy and see if it helps convince you (or your board) of the importance of fundraising.

The "New Economy"

Ah, the good old days. Back when the government had plenty of money to help organizations, United Way was for everyone, corporations were good corporate citizens, and foundations expected only a letter of request. Back in those days, you could be a small organization with few individual donors and still have some chance of being funded because foundations and corporations gave away money to a broad spectrum of organizations. But, alas, those days are no more. In the present economy, the government is no longer a reliable payer because federal, state, and local governments are all feeling the pinch and cutting back on investments in services for the most needy. United Way narrowed its funding to specific community issues it deems a priority or even creating and funding its own programs to meet them. Corporations no longer give to a variety of organizations but have narrowed their focus to things that help them meet their missions or develop their bottom lines. And foundations have high expectations in an ever more competitive environment for funding and expect high-impact outcomes as a return on their investments. That leaves only individual donors. Fortunately, individual giving in the United States has remained fairly steady over the last several decades.

Old Economy	New Economy
Government was a reliable source of grant funding or a reliable third-party payer.	Government cutbacks mean greater competition, stagnant reimbursement rates, or limited slots for the most needy.
United Way served most organizations in the community but was usually "the only game in town" for payroll deduction giving.	United Way focuses on key community issues it deems a priority, creates and funds its own programs, or has an RFP process that sometimes pushes out former funding recipients. New organizations similar in function to United Way have sprung up to fill the void, but sometimes access is limited to certain types of organizations, such as health related, etc.
Foundations gave to many different organizations and responded to simple requests.	Competition is fierce and lofty outcomes are expected in order to receive funding. Online applications, letter of intent processes, and stringent requirements have replaced older standards.
Corporations gave because it was the right thing to do and supported a variety of organizations in the community.	Corporations give to targeted initiatives and want to see a return on investment to prove the worth of their philanthropic projects to their stockholders and investors.
Individuals gave readily through phone solicitation, direct mail, televised appeals, special events, and personal appeals.	Individuals still give but want to control the amount of solicitations they receive or seek to direct their giving to specific projects or programs where they can be personally involved.

But let's say you're one of those organizations that has relied on government funding as your primary source of income through federal, state, county grant, or block grant funds. Maybe your organization is one that used to qualify for United Way funding or funding from such sources as pharmaceutical companies. Bottom line: you've never needed to develop relationships with individuals, and now the other funding streams are drying up. You're trapped in the new economy. If you haven't been preparing for it, you've been caught unaware, and now that it's here, you need help but don't know where to begin. Unfortunately, you aren't alone.

Swimming in a Red Ocean

Why unfortunately? Because, as the book *Blue Ocean Strategy* describes it, you are swimming in a red ocean. The ocean of potential funding sources is red with the blood of competition from other organizations, all of which are vying for the same small piece of the proverbial pie, and guess what? All of these organizations are also clamoring for the attention of individual donors. The organizations that already know how to fundraise are leaving no stone unturned, building their infrastructures and increasing their communications to donors so that donors stay engaged and involved. That leaves the organizations that never began creating relationships in the community even farther behind.

I cannot emphasize this enough: it is imperative that your organization strengthen its fundraising skill set and build relationships with individual donors. The competition is simply too fierce for you to do otherwise. Nonprofits that fail to do this do not survive.

I know this news may be alarming, and I wish I could tell you the fundraising process was going to be easy or that it would happen overnight. It won't. The good news is that you can start to prepare your organization today, and you can begin with the basic building blocks of fundraising success.

To Recap

- Fundraising is more than just asking people for money; fundraising changes the world by connecting donors' passions with organizations' missions.
- Professional fundraising involves utilizing proven methods and techniques that strengthen donors' relationships with the organization.
- Fundraising is imperative for nonprofit organizations in today's "new economy," and those that are not schooled in fundraising will be left behind.
- Successful fundraising can be achieved by putting the right building blocks in place.

Chapter Two

The First of the Four Building Blocks of Fundraising Success

IN THIS CHAPTER

- Discover the four building blocks to fundraising success
- Learn why donors don't want to put water into a leaky bucket
- Understand why your board and CEO can make or break your fundraising success
- Find out what your development staff really needs to succeed
- Uncover the secrets in your backroom operations

Before a house is built, a foundation must be laid. That foundation must be strong, watertight, and made with high-quality materials. The same thing is true for your nonprofit organization as it begins a fundraising program. You must build a strong foundation for success by ensuring that all the key materials, or "building blocks," are in place. If a block is missing, costly problems may occur that bring down the whole structure.

In the next several chapters, I will introduce the basic building blocks of successful fundraising. The blocks are:

- organizational readiness;
- fundraising goals and plans;
- primary fundraising vehicles; and
- communications and community relations.

All four of these building blocks are important components of any successful fundraising venture and are important for your organization to understand and invest in. Simply put: your efforts may not be successful if one of these building blocks is missing. So let's get started!

Building Block One: Organizational Readiness

Organizational readiness is the foundation of fundraising success, like the foundation of a house. A nonprofit with critical deficits, just like a house with a cracked foundation, will find it very challenging to build a successful organization. Financial stability, a board of trustees with high capacity that is prepared to fulfill its duties, a CEO with an understanding of fundraising and good connections in the community, a well-prepared and seasoned development staff, and sufficient backroom operations are the hallmarks of organizational readiness.

Financial Stability

The very first thing you must know in order to be successful at fundraising is that you cannot put more water into a leaky bucket. What I mean by this is that before attempting to raise funds, you need to be sure that you are already as financially secure as you can be. The business side of your organization must be running, if not ideally, then to the best of its ability, before you ask the community to invest in your organization. Donors and funders want to see that you have done everything you can to create sustainable programs with sufficient revenue streams, lean but effective operations, and— if applicable—a safe and well-maintained physical plant. In other words, fundraising cannot be your saving grace. If at all possible, your goal should be self-sustainment for all programs. Fundraising dollars should be used as "icing on the cake" for program expansion, unmet needs, or capital improvements. You may be able to attract donations for an emergency need, but emergency fundraising cannot be your modus operandi long term.

To get a feel for where your organization stands in this area, complete the worksheet on the following page. This may require a conversation with your CFO. (Note: if you don't have the information to complete the worksheet or this information doesn't exist, consider that a red flag. This kind of information is crucial for strategic planning and should be readily available, at least to your CFO and CEO.)

On the left column, list all your current programs, i.e., the services you provide to the community. For each program, consider its primary income source. Is it a reliable source? How much do you receive versus how much it actually costs to run the program? What percentage of the costs, if any, are not covered? Now, if there are uncovered costs, what are they? Are they administrative costs, such as salaries, benefits, or overhead? Are they direct costs, such as supplies and materials? Based on this assessment, can you determine any untapped sources that might cover those costs?

Knowing which of your programs are running in the red helps you identify your fundraising needs, but it also indicates how big the "hole" is in your "bucket." If the "hole" is significant, stop here. Before you begin fundraising, you need to plug the hole and undertake the hard work of becoming financially stable.

Assessment of Financial Stability

Assess each program using the table provided.

Programs	Income Source(s)	Are These Sources Reliable?	Approximate Annual Revenue for This Program	Approximate Costs of This Program	What Percentage of the Costs of This Program Is Not Covered?	Specifically What Kinds of Costs Are Incurred by This Program?	Are There Untapped Sources to Cover Uncovered Costs?	What Would Be Required to Tap These Resources?

1. Does your organization have an operating reserve or investments?
2. Is there an endowment? If so, how much? How old is it?
3. Consider your answers to the last two columns in your program assessment. What is your plan for tapping untapped resources?

Use the table below to help design a plan.

Program	Need	Basic Plan

Becoming financially stable may require you or your organization's leadership to make difficult choices. It may require cutting poor-performing programs, increasing expectations around staff productivity, moving into a smaller or more affordable location, or any of a number of other decisions. But in the end, your organization must be able to show that it is doing all it can to continue to fulfill its mission in the most efficient and effective way possible. Donors need to see that your leadership is strong and capable of taking bold steps to ensure the organization's future. Then and only then will others want to invest their philanthropic dollars in your organization.

> Remember when we talked about "those organizations" that seem to get all the donations and PR? I can guarantee you that those organizations have strong boards. Warning: this may be painful, but you need to know. If your organization has a board of well-meaning, mission-focused do-nothings, your organization will not be successful at fundraising. If the board is focused on the day-to-day operations of the organization instead of the big picture, your organization will not be successful at fundraising. If the board members have few connections or do not make personal donations, your organization will not be successful at fundraising.
>
> **watch out!**

Board of Directors Capacity/Preparedness

The second and equally important part of organizational readiness is the capacity and preparedness of your board of directors or trustees. (You should refer to your board depending on how it is described in your bylaws.) There are many resources available to help organizations strengthen their boards, and I have recommended some of these in **Appendix B**. Here again is the bottom line: the stronger your board, the stronger your ability to raise funds.

So what does a good fundraising board look like? It is composed of people of influence and/or affluence, is diverse in age, gender, race, and skill set, and—depending on your organization's mission—is diverse in socioeconomic status. (You should have some client representation on your board if possible.) They should believe fiercely in your mission, be able to articulate the mission and the vision as ambassadors in the community, and be willing to extend both their personal finances and their social capital to assist the organization. Finally, as a group, they must spend time and energy on the big picture, "steering the ship" of the organization and assisting the CEO in making strategic decisions.

If that description sounds exactly like your board or even something like your board, great! Probably with a few improvements, you'll be well on your way to fundraising success. If it sounds nothing like your board, then my suggestion is that you create a governance committee to review the board's structure and performance and arrange for board training as soon as possible. Many community foundations and some private foundations provide funding for just that type of capacity-building activity.

Nonperforming boards are...	Performing boards are...	What to do about it
Well-meaning "do-nothings" with no connections	People of influence and affluence	Create/empower a board governance or nominating committee; create a trustee prospect list; begin replacing members slowly as seats become open; identify a champion/leader to attract new blood.
All one race, gender, sexual orientation, age, religion, or political persuasion; no consumers	Diverse with at least one consumer	Complete a board matrix; governance committee targets prospects.
Not sure exactly what the organization does or how it helps the community and can't explain it to others	Ambassadors capable of articulating the mission and vision to the community	Work with a consultant or development staff to provide the correct language and helpful collaterals; train members on programs at each meeting; require volunteering in programs.
Bogged down in day-to-day operations; long, tedious meetings	Steering the ship, focusing on big picture issues; sixty- to ninety-minute meetings, often using a consent agenda	Conduct board training; use a consent agenda; use committee meetings between full board meetings to complete action items.
Not giving personally or asking others to give and don't feel like they know how	Embracing their fundraising role	Conduct board fundraising training; empower development staff to guide/ prod board members.

CEO Fundraising Knowledge and Community Connectedness

Your board is crucial to fundraising success. Yet in many ways, the community will judge your organization by your CEO, not by your board. It's for this reason that your CEO must be a competent, credible, highly moral person who represents your organization in a positive way in the community and who is "seen." In other words, your CEO must spend at least 30 to 40 percent of the workweek being involved in the community on committees, civic groups, etc., that benefit the organization and make it more visible. Why is this important to your fundraising success? Because if your CEO is spending too much time putting out fires in the organization and working in the office, then your organization's chief fundraiser is not out in the community building relationships that will benefit the organization. And if that isn't happening, your organization isn't on the radar of people who give.

Myth versus Reality

Myth: The CEO shouldn't be involved in finding prospects for the board.

Reality: The CEO must be involved with this process with the guidance and blessing of a board nominating or governance committee. This group (CEO and nominating committee) also takes responsibility for orienting new board members.

Myth: It's impossible to get a board that has never raised funds to begin raising them.

Reality: It's definitely hard work, but you can change the culture of your board to embrace philanthropy through training, peer pressure, and strategic replacement of difficult board members.

Myth: You can't fire a board member.

Reality: It's the job of the board chair or nominating chair to speak with nonparticipating or difficult board members and encourage them to rotate off the board if necessary. If neither chairperson will do the job, then it becomes much more difficult to accomplish.

Development Staff Preparedness

There are many organizations that do not have full-time fundraising staff. Some organizations have development staff that previously served as administrative staff or social workers/program staff. You may be just such a person. There is nothing wrong with this choice as long as these individuals receive training in professional fundraising techniques and best practices. An organization cannot expect anyone who does not know how to do the job effectively to be successful in the job—and that goes for fundraising too. If you want your organization to be successful at fundraising, then fundraising cannot be a last-minute, low-priority activity done by people who don't know what they are doing. It requires an investment of time and talent, plain and simple, just like any other part of your organization.

If you are the person who has never raised funds but is now expected to do so, the first thing you should do is connect with your local chapter of the Association of Fundraising Professionals. This group offers ongoing educational seminars, training, and conferences, as well as ready-reference materials and personal support from colleagues. Secondly, check out the fundraising titles available through CharityChannel Press or For the GENIUS Press. Well-known, seasoned fundraising professionals from around the country write these books.

Another way to get the talent you need for less money is to hire a consultant or contractor. You can hire someone with a great deal of experience on a project or retainer basis for much less than a full-time staff person or even a part-time person with limited or no experience. You can also hire that person to train or coach your CEO or staff so that they can be more successful without a huge outlay of expenses for training.

Backroom Operations

The last piece of the puzzle for fundraising readiness is your backroom operations. What do I mean by that? I'm referring to the tasks that must be covered by staff or volunteers, such as processing checks, writing thank-you notes, and maintaining the donor database. Here is a list of what you need for your back room:

- A donor database. This can be as simple as an Excel file or as elaborate as licensed software or anything in between. Whatever you use, just remember: junk in equals junk out. Your data must be clean, coded in a simple and consistent way, and updated regularly. A database is more than just a list. It's your "institutional memory," allowing you to work more efficiently and effectively to build successful donor relationships.

- Someone in charge of the database who is zealous about the cleanliness of the data. In other words, database management can't be left to an administrative worker with too many additional duties. Ideally, this job is given to someone as that person's primary work.

- A process for acknowledging gifts within twenty-four to forty-eight hours of receiving them. Sometimes this is harder for small shops because it doesn't seem like it's worth the effort to write thank-you letters one or two at a time. Make it a priority to respond as quickly as you can, with the goal of forty-eight hours maximum. Believe me, donors are impressed by this small act!

- Written fundraising policies and procedures. Chief among these is a check-processing procedure that ensures more than one person sees or handles the checks for auditing purposes. Another important one is a gift-acceptance policy detailing what the organization will or won't accept in the way of gifts and why. This is normally developed by staff and approved by the board.

- Good, reliable donor reports. You must be able to create reports on who has given, how much, and when, and they must be accurate so that donor lists can be made for your annual report. This is where "the rubber meets the road" for database cleanliness. If your database if full of junk, you'll know it when you run a report.

Now use the following table to assess where your organization stands in terms of its backroom operations and consider what steps you need to take to put basic operations in place.

Backroom Operations Assessment

Operation	Basic Needs	Your Current Status
Donor database	An easy-to-learn, affordable database product that can be tailored for your organization's needs and grow with you as you add more donors	
Database manager	A competent person who has primary responsibility for the content of the database and is able to provide needed reports	
Acknowledgment process	A written policy or procedure that states who will write thank-you letters and how quickly they will be sent	
Development policies/ procedures	Check-cashing procedure, acknowledgment procedure, database procedures, gift-acceptance policy	
Database reports	Your database manager should be able to utilize your database to create reports of: (1) who has given what, when, and for what purpose; (2) giving to specific initiatives or timeframes; (3) donors by certain variables, such as where they live or some other classification	

To Recap

- Organizations must be financially stable in order for donors to feel comfortable giving.
- Your board must be diverse, understand its fiduciary duty, and embrace its role as chief ambassador for the organization.
- Your CEO must spend time cultivating relationships in the community.
- Your development staff needs to be qualified and trained.
- A reliable donor database and backroom procedures are more important than you realize.

Chapter Three

Building Block Two: Fundraising Goals and Plans

IN THIS CHAPTER

- Learn how your strategic plan lays a foundation for success in fundraising
- Tell your organization's story through your case for support
- Build a basic fundraising plan

If you or your organization is new to fundraising, then sitting down to create a plan for your fundraising efforts is critical. The three key steps to creating fundraising goals and plans are: (1) create a strategic plan and use it as the guide; (2) craft the arguments as to why others should support your mission; and (3) build a solicitation plan that will produce the results you are seeking.

Your Strategic Plan

Perhaps it seems like an overstatement to claim that a nonprofit organization is lost without a strategic plan. But I believe, and have seen firsthand, that this rule is absolutely true. Small organizations that are struggling to continue to provide service and just keep their heads above water financially often look at larger, more successful organizations and wonder how they do it. The answer is a plan. These successful organizations have a plan for what they want to be when they grow up, and they have a strategic approach for how they are going to get there. These organizations also implement the plan. Each subsequent decision about programs, staff, physical plant, or fundraising initiatives is weighed against the plan and how the choice will advance the organization's ultimate goals.

While there are many approaches to strategic planning and every organization must determine the best course for itself, I found one of the best ideas for a starting point to strategic planning is an exercise that involves imagining the future and dreaming about what others might say about your organization in twenty years or more.

Let's take a few moments and do that now.

It's twenty years from now. You find an article online about the great work being done in your organization. The article highlights your organization's history of innovation and the impact of the programs on the community, and it tells a story of a person who triumphed over adversity, thanks to your intervention. Pretend you're the article's author and write it below.

Hopefully this exercise gets you started by dreaming of what you want to happen. What does your organization want to be when it grows up? What is the vision of what you hope to achieve in the world? From here, it's a simple matter of determining a strategic path that will get you to your destination. That path may begin with getting your house in order. Fundraising is likely to be one of those high-priority items. In fact, you may find that your first strategic plan includes goals based on the deficits you discovered in your organization after reading this book.

If you don't know where to begin, have a conversation with a consultant. There are many available in your area. You may find you have some work to do before you actually begin strategic planning. Whatever you do, don't fail to make a plan, because whatever you do may fail.

If you undertake a strategic plan, here are several traps to avoid:

- Trap one: involving your whole board for the whole process. Create a committee of a few board members, staff, and key community constituents, especially for the preplanning phase. While it's critical to have the whole board involved in one or two sessions, involving the whole board in all the sessions will only bog down the process, especially if you have a large board.

- Trap two: leaving with a two-page summary. Some consultants prepare a final report from your planning sessions and summarize it in a one- to four-page document. This will do you little good. Be sure your strategic plan has actionable items and an implementation process included in the final product.

- Trap three: sticking it on a shelf. You could spend $10,000 to $50,000 on a strategic plan that makes everyone feel great but is quickly put on a shelf when everyone gets back to their day-to-day work. This is probably the worst trap of all. Your organization's leadership must incorporate forward movement on the strategic plan into daily operations and report on this progress regularly to the board and staff.

Your Case for Support

In order for a piece of music to be performed properly, everyone in the orchestra must be using the same sheet music. Otherwise, it will sound discordant or out of sync. The same is true in nonprofit organizations.

A critical part of fundraising success is a document containing everything an organization needs in order to explain itself to potential donors. This is called a case for support (or "case" for short). According to the Association of Fundraising Professionals, "the case is the expression of the cause and all the reasons why prospective donors might want to contribute to the advancement of the cause." A case is used for many reasons, including fundraising materials, grant proposals, marketing materials, and speeches. Nonprofit staff members and board members will use this document when they are discussing the organization in the community or with potential donors. Without the case for support, an organization's fundraising requests can seem disorganized and poorly managed.

A case for support contains the following basic items:

- Basic organizational information
- *Brief* history
- Mission statement/primary goal
- Vision and impact statements

- Organizational values
- Program description
- Needs statement
- Objectives
- Outcomes
- Evaluation measures
- Financial information
- Leadership information

Also be sure to have the following on hand: an IRS designation letter, Form 990, audit, operational budget, and individual program budgets. It also helps to keep copies of letters of support or articles about your work.

Use this worksheet to get started on collecting what you need to write a case for support.

Item	Notes on Status of Items
I. Basic Organizational Information Collect the following information: ◆ Organization name ◆ Address ◆ Phone ◆ Web address ◆ Primary contact (usually the CEO or executive director) ◆ Primary contact information ◆ Secondary contact (usually the person responsible for managing a project) ◆ Secondary contact information	
II. Brief history Include a brief statement of the historical highlights of your organization. Avoid bullet points, and try to show how your organization has changed, grown, or improved to meet current demands.	

Item	Notes on Status of Items
III. Mission Statement/Primary Goal This is the place for your mission statement or, if it's too cumbersome, a restatement of it as a "primary goal" for the organization. You may have both if you wish.	
IV. Vision and Impact Statements What is the vision of your organization? What do you want to be when you "grow up"? What do you expect to happen in the community or the world in ten-plus years if your goals are met? State your vision or impact in as few sentences as possible.	
V. Organizational Values What are the key values of your organization? Try to describe them in as few words as possible. A great way is to come up with specific words that embody the spirit of your mission and then define them based on your vision and impact.	
VI. Program Description Specifically, what programs do you provide? Whom do they serve? Where do they take place? Who performs them? This can be a list with a brief description for each program that includes this information.	
VII. Needs Statement Collect evidence as to your community's needs and why the programs you provide are necessary to meet those needs. Also discuss why you do your programs in the way that you do. Write an essay about this that convinces the reader why your organization's programs are worthy of support, and utilize statistics and other research to back up your claims. This is the most important part of the case for support.	
VIII. Objectives What are the ways in which you go about obtaining your primary goal? This is not a list of programs but of what the programs set out to accomplish.	
IX. Outcomes What are the changes that are expected if those objectives are fulfilled? This is a list of what the programs actually, quantifiably accomplish.	

Item	Notes on Status of Items
X. Evaluation Measures How do you show that your work is effective? Specify what tools you use to show effectiveness. Be certain these tools actually measure your program objectives.	
XI. Financial Information Provide basic income and expense information that shows how much of your income is spent on programs. A great way to do this is by using charts, graphs, or tables.	
XII. Leadership Information Include a board list with name, title, and affiliation. Create short executive staff bios of a paragraph in length.	

Your Fundraising Plans

Earlier we talked about the strategic plan. Now we must address its sister, the fundraising plan. The fundraising plan must go hand in hand with the strategic plan. Fundraising must be approached strategically for the greatest success and to truly benefit the long-term mission of the organization. This also means that development staff members need to be involved in the strategic planning process. CEOs need to understand the importance of this, and development staff members need to advocate to be included in the planning.

> You may have heard the term "case for support" or "case statement" if you were involved in a capital campaign, especially for a university or college. In a capital campaign, the case is often a slick brochure or notebook of information provided to potential donors. Just remember, a case for support is a collection of documents and does not have to be in the form of an expensive brochure. It does help to have those documents merged into one edited and formatted document, however. This proves to be very helpful when sharing it with potential donors and funders.

A fundraising plan includes the vehicles you want to use for fundraising, the timeframe for completing them, the amount that each should raise, and an estimate for what can be raised in subsequent years (percentage increase expected over time). The plan may also require explanations about staffing and costs.

Creating a Fundraising Plan

Fundraising plans usually include three major components: a plan for soliciting donors (including identifying them), a plan for cultivating donor relationships (including stewarding existing donors), and a plan for managing donor information. Since donor relations, communications, and backroom operations are covered in other areas of this manual, we will focus on solicitation here.

Solicitation Plan

First, ask the following key questions. Research your answers if necessary since everything you do will be based on the answers to these questions:

- What do we need to raise money for and/or what is needed in the marketplace? (Make sure these are justifiable needs that can be backed up with evidence of the need.)
- How much do we need to raise for each identified priority?
- How much of an investment is the board willing to make to raise the necessary dollars (seed money)?

Once you have determined your needs, consider what resources you have at your disposal from which to raise funds. Be as thorough as you can in your search. Be brutally honest.

Resource	Yes	No	Details
Board of trustee contacts/connections			
Executive staff contacts/connections			
Volunteers			
Individual donors			
Local foundations			
Local corporations			
Local clubs, organizations, or congregations			
Government funding			
Special events			
Fee for service activities			
Entrepreneurial activities (business income)			
Other			

Determine which of these resources can be utilized to create specific fundraising activities. Use this table as a guide.

Resource	Fundraising Activity
Board of trustee contacts/connections	Board campaigns
Executive staff contacts/connections	Create a guest list and invite contacts in for tours
Volunteers	Volunteer campaign
Individual donors	Annual campaigns, major gift campaigns, online giving, staff campaigns
Local foundations	Grant proposal writing
Local corporations	Grant proposal writing, event sponsorship, face-to-face business appeal
Local clubs, organizations, or congregations	Community speaking engagements and grant proposal writing
Government funding	Grant proposal writing
Special events	Luncheons, dinners, auctions, sporting events, concerts, etc.
Entrepreneurial activities (business income)	Janitorial services, thrift stores, catering businesses, etc.

Next, consider what budget you have to cover the expenses of those activities. Based on your expense budget, decide which activities you can afford to undertake. Once you have done this, create a budget for each activity of expected income for the next two to three years and expected expenses. Be sure to include the cost of any new staff, staff training, or backroom needs (such as a donor database) you may need to complete the plan.

To Recap

- Often the difference between a high-functioning successful nonprofit and one that is struggling is a strategic vision clearly spelled out in a strategic plan.
- The case for support identifies exactly why donors should give to your organization and becomes the rallying point for everyone who works for or on behalf of the organization.
- A fundraising plan is necessary for assessing fundraising progress and should relate directly to the strategic plan and case for support.

Chapter Four

Building Block Three: Primary Fundraising Vehicles

IN THIS CHAPTER

- Discover what constitutes an annual giving program
- Uncover the difference between a friend-raising event and a fundraising event
- Find out how you can successfully solicit foundations and corporations
- Learn how to implement a basic planned giving program

In order to determine if your organization is ready for fundraising, you need to know the basic tools of the trade. This chapter will give you a quick look at each of the main fundraising vehicles. You'll also gain insight as to whether your organization can effectively implement these vehicles.

Annual Giving

Annual giving comprises those activities most often undertaken by nonprofit organizations (activities your organization may already be doing): mail campaigns, phone campaigns, email campaigns, etc. In other words, annual giving is asking individuals for a specific amount of money, usually for a general operating purpose. It's important that every organization consider how it can implement basic annual giving techniques, especially since this is often the primary source of general operating dollars.

But whom should you ask? Where does the list come from? Who should do the asking? How often should you ask and for how much? These are all critical questions for organizations just starting to create an annual giving program.

In the previous worksheet, you were asked to determine what your needs are for fundraising. Most likely your list included general operating needs otherwise known as unrestricted funds. Because individuals are the most reliable source of unrestricted funds, it's best to focus your annual giving program on operating needs. But first you must determine whom you are going to ask and how. This worksheet will walk you through the steps for determining your donor base and deciding what vehicles to use for soliciting them.

Step One: Determine Your Universe of Prospective Donors

Each organization has a different universe of prospective individual donors. Your first job, therefore, is to determine your universe. Here are some suggestions:

- Board members
- Former board members
- Advisory board members
- Volunteers
- Staff
- Former staff (on good terms with the organization)
- Previous donors
- In-kind gift donors
- Special event attendees
- Family of bequest donors
- Clients/alumni/patients
- Family of former or current clients/alumni/patients
- Community members interested in your cause
- People on any mailing lists who have not given previously

Step Two: Make a List

The next step is to create a prospect database of contact information. This is a *huge* and *imperative* step for conducting annual campaigns. Begin by using a basic spreadsheet to create your database.

The column headings of your spreadsheet should be:

- Last name
- First name
- Maiden name (if applicable)
- Nickname
- Credentials
- Organization
- Street address
- City
- State
- Zip
- Phone one
- Phone two
- Email
- Facebook account name
- Twitter account name
- Most recent gift amount
- Date of most recent gift
- Largest gift amount
- Date of largest gift amount
- How gift was given (what vehicle)
- Special code one
- Special code two

You will populate the rows of your spreadsheet with your donor's information. Make sure you separate the address from the city, state, and zip code so you can manipulate this information better. The special codes are ones you design for your own purposes based on whatever information is pertinent to your work or your fundraising program.

Step Three: Segment Your Donors

When it comes to solicitations, personalization is best. So segment your data any way that you can to create affinity groups: people who have common characteristics and/or motivations for becoming involved in your organization. Because this will be different for every organization, you will need to determine these for yourself. These groups can be regrouped to receive the same solicitations, but it's a good exercise to analyze your data in this way. The better you know who your donors are, the better the chances of being successful soliciting them. Here are some suggested segmentations:

Common Segmentations for Donors
Date of last gift
Size of gift
How gift was given
Reason for involvement in your organization
Age
Location
Level of influence or affluence

Step Four: Choose the Best Vehicles to Solicit Your Donors

Use the following table as a guide. Your choices will likely be determined by your budget.

Type of Donor	Possible Annual Giving Vehicle
Well-to-do or influential board members, former board members, volunteers, advisory board members, or community members	Private gatherings with the CEO in homes, a restaurant, or a private tour/luncheon on-site
Volunteers	Key volunteer leader makes request through a letter
Staff	Staff campaigns or workplace campaigns
Previous donors	Call from the CEO or letter from the board chair; newsletter with solicitation envelope; annual report with solicitation envelope; phone-a-thon
All other potential donors	Letter from the board chair or a local celebrity; newsletter with solicitation envelope; annual report with solicitation envelope; phone-a-thon
Younger donors	Online giving, Twitter, Pinterest, and/or Facebook
Board contacts (prospective donors)	Board campaign (i.e., board members asking their contacts for support; some organizations also include the annual solicitation of board members into this definition)

Step Five: Design Your Vehicles

Designing your annual giving vehicles is one of the more challenging aspects of putting together an annual campaign. The best and most economical thing to do is look at what other organizations are doing in terms of their mail solicitations, online solicitations, newsletters, annual reports, websites, Facebook pages, etc. Then gather a team of volunteers and a good in-house designer at a local printing company to help you design your campaigns and determine the timeline for sending them out.

Special Events

Most professional fundraisers will tell you that special events are a necessary evil. They are necessary because they are one of the most effective ways for getting the word out about your cause, engaging new prospective donors in your organization, and attracting media attention to your organization. They are evil because they are the most time-consuming and expensive way to raise money. I would add that they are also evil because they are the default fundraising vehicle preferred by many boards of small organizations, which results in overtaxing an already-overworked staff. For this reason, I urge caution when considering special events. I believe that small organizations should have no less than one and no more than three per year, with two as the best number.

If you do not have special events or you have too many, consider creating or cutting back to two events: a fundraising event and a friend-raising event. In other words, one event that will raise money for the organization while simultaneously building awareness and one event that will build awareness while simultaneously raising money. Aren't they the same? Not quite. Staff and boards undertake a fundraising event knowing that raising the budgeted dollar amount is the stated goal. The outcome of a friend-raising event is measured differently: by ambassadors made, influential people or donors cultivated, or mission advanced or celebrated. Approaching your events this way helps alleviate the pressure but still raises the status of your organization in the community, both as one worth giving to and as one worth sharing. Take a look at the following table to help determine the difference.

People Give to People

When it's all said and done, people give to people. Donors must believe that their donations are being given to a person who is trustworthy. That person may be you, your CEO, a board member, or a volunteer. Your job is to make sure that your donors—new or old—continue to believe in your organization and continue to have a relationship with your organization via their key contact. This is what annual giving achieves if done correctly: ongoing support of your mission from people who trust you, your CEO, and your board to invest it wisely.

principle

	Fundraising Event	Friend-Raising Event
Goal	To raise funds.	To advance the mission.
Objective/Purpose	To host a public or private event that offers participants an opportunity to give, usually in a transactional manner.	To host a public or private event that educates the public about the organization's mission or impact and offers an opportunity to give, usually in a relational manner, i.e., participants choose to begin a relationship with the organization or share their concern for your cause by asking others to get involved.
Outcome	Supporters and their guests have fun and raise dollars for the organization.	Supporters and guests are inspired to help the organization and get involved.
Examples	Traditional galas, auctions, dances, dinners, award luncheons, sporting events, etc., where participants pay an entry fee of some kind or purchase items.	Community events, open houses, health fairs, or any event in which the primary activity is learning about the organization or raising public awareness.

I mentioned that when considering a special event, your organization should proceed with caution. This is because special events are notorious for taking a lot of staff time and sometimes netting very little. To be sure that your event is actually raising money for your organization, you need to conduct a cost/benefit analysis. How do you do it? Keep track of *all* your expenses, including your staff's time and your volunteers' time. Make sure you keep track of the value of in-kind donations too. Then create a spreadsheet that includes the income derived from the event, sponsorships, ticket sales, in-kind donations, and the like. In a separate table, show all the true costs, including the value of your time and your volunteers' time. Determine how much it cost you to raise each dollar. If it's less than twenty-five cents, you're doing fine. More than that could mean you're spending too much to raise too little. And that doesn't even begin to measure the frustration and exhaustion!

Before you begin, gather the following information:

Cost/Benefit Analysis Worksheet	
Each staff person who worked on the event	
Each staff person's hourly rate	
Total cost of staff	
Number of full-time staff with benefits	
Cost of benefits per eligible staff member (usually 28 percent of salary)	
Number of hours worked by each staff person	
Hourly cost of benefits for each full-time staff person	
Number of volunteers	
Number of hours worked by volunteers	

Now use this information to complete the following calculations:

Revenue	Amount	Explanation
Donations		Any cash donations over and above ticket sales
Ticket sales		Total amount received from individual ticket sales
Sponsorships		Total amount received from sponsors
Purchased items		Amount raised from auction or other items purchased at the event
In-kind donations		Dollar value of donated goods and services
Total income		Total amount raised

Expenses	Amount	Explanation
Direct costs of event		The actual cost of doing the event (venue, food, decorations, etc.)
◆ Direct cost one		List each cost category separately
◆ Direct cost two		
◆ Direct cost three		
Indirect costs of campaign (see list above)		Other associated costs of doing the event, such as staff
◆ Salaries		
◆ Benefits		
◆ Volunteer value		
Total expenses		The total of all direct and indirect costs
Net revenue		The total income minus the direct costs
True net		The total income minus total expenses

Special Giving and Major Giving

If you are fortunate enough to have a database of individual donors, then you can begin to ask for special and major gifts. What do I mean by those terms? Special gifts are usually one-time gifts for a specific purpose, such as a piece of equipment, a renovation, or a new program. These gifts may come from a donor's income or assets and be given in addition to an annual gift. Major gifts are also given for a specific purpose but are always given out of a donor's assets and usually over a period of time.

Another difference between annual gifts and major or special gifts is how they are solicited. Annual gifts can be solicited any number of ways, including mail, phone, email, or even social media. Major gifts are solicited face to face. This is because of the decision-making process that I previously referenced. People considering a major gift need a great deal of cultivation in order to come to that decision and may need to involve others, such as spouses, family members, lawyers, or financial planners.

If you would like to learn how to solicit major gifts, I highly recommend you take a course specifically focused on this, such as the one offered by the Institute of Charitable Giving operated by Jerold Panas, Linzy & Partners. To see if you are ready to begin a major gifts program, consider the following:

- Step one: determine the projects requiring support. Before you can ask anyone for a gift, you need to know what projects you have for consideration. This step may require discussions with other executive-level staff of your organization. Gather as much detailed information about these projects as possible.

- Step two: develop "the case" for these projects. Potential donors are going to want to know why they should support your initiative or project. Do your homework by creating a needs statement for each project and incorporating it into your existing case for support. (In other words, create a tailored case for support for each project.)

- Step three: determine if you have any major gift donors. If you have donors who have given consistently over time, have significant assets, and have shown a passion for your cause, then you have major gift prospects. If you don't know anyone fitting this description, then wait until you do to launch a major gift program and seek funding from corporations and foundations first instead.

Defining Major Gifts

I've heard fundraisers say that "a major gift is different for every organization and can be defined as any gift that is large enough to make a significant difference to your organization." By this definition, a major gift may be $1,000 for some and $100,000 for others. I asked this question to one of the grandfathers of major giving, Kent E. Dove of Indiana University, and he replied that this is not true. Major gifts are defined as gifts given from assets, for a special purpose, over time. Usually $1,000 gifts—even if that is a significant gift to your organization—are just large annual gifts, not major gifts. The best way to think about it is this: annual gifts require only a moderate level of thought on the part of the donor; major gifts require a great deal of thought. No matter the dollar amount, the difference is the thought process required to give the gift.

food for thought

Planned Giving

Planned giving are gifts made by a donor during the donor's lifetime that usually benefit an organization after the donor's death. This may include a designation in a will, trust, life insurance, or other vehicles. It is not the job of any fundraising professional to help a donor determine estate plans, but it is helpful to have a working knowledge of planned giving vehicles. If you don't have time for this, however, you can still have a planned giving program by simply identifying those who wish to benefit you in their estate plans and asking them to tell you so.

The easiest way to do this is to ask in a newsletter or even to send out a special mailing asking your constituents to let you know if they have remembered your organization in their estate plans.

Corporate and Foundation Relations

Although over 80 percent of gifts given in the United States are given by individuals, it behooves every nonprofit organization to uncover the companies and foundations in their geographic area that may be able to assist them through grants or other forms of corporate support. In fact, you may find these donors to be more approachable and more lucrative when first starting a fundraising program.

There are two important rules to remember before launching a corporate/foundation relations program (otherwise known as grantwriting):

- Rule one: do your homework. Never apply to a company or foundation that doesn't have a mission that matches your mission unless you have a relationship with a board member or family member (of a family foundation).

> Many small shops or novice fundraisers find planned giving to be more than they can handle. In fact, this is a common issue for social service nonprofits. To find ideas about how to develop a simple planned giving program, go to leavealegacy.org.
>
> **food for thought**

- Rule two: treat your corporate and foundation funders like other donors. This means that they need to be cultivated like other donors and that you should develop a relationship with key personnel at the company or foundation. Visit them annually.

If your organization does not already have a corporate/foundation relations program, then here is a step-by-step guide for creating one:

- Step one: the first step is research. Identify the private and publicly held corporations and the private or corporate foundations that give in your area by visiting your local library or using one of many online tools.

- Step two: determine if their interests match what you do. Then call for an appointment with the community relations officer or foundation relationship manager. Take materials describing what you do and your current needs (be as specific as possible), and be prepared to answer questions about your organization. It's great to take a board member along as well, or even a program director.

- Step three: ask what you must do to apply. Then be sure you follow their guidelines to the letter.

- Step four: return each year for a visit, and send newsletters or other publications to the organization throughout the year. Never contact a corporate or foundation funder only once a year when soliciting support.

Once you have determined your pool of prospects, create a database of information, including their basic contact information, the name of any key personnel you've had contact with, the types of grants they give, the purposes for which they give, due dates, and any information about their past giving to your organization, if applicable. Finally, be sure the due dates of any grant proposals, the required reports, and visits to key corporate/foundation personnel are part of your master calendar of fundraising activities.

If you have never researched grants, it may be helpful to know the following definitions of the most common types of foundations:

- Private foundation: a trust established by a founder or set of founders for an established charitable purpose and governed by a group of private citizens or family members. Examples include community foundations or national foundations and trusts.
- Corporate foundation: fund established by a corporation for the purpose of acting on its charitable initiatives. Many large companies have several avenues for giving, including marketing/sponsorship, in-kind donations, and philanthropic giving through a charitable giving program other than the foundation. These different avenues often require different relationships and solicitation processes.
- Public funder: any public entity (federal government, states, counties, etc.) that creates RFPs in order to complete work established through federal or state legislation. Examples include county governments, state governments, and the federal government.

Foundations or corporations can be very different in the way they distribute funding. It's important to know what kind of funder a foundation or corporation is before you request funding. Following are the different types of funders:

- National or international in scope: foundations that are national or international in scope tend to look for demonstration projects, i.e., projects that are making a significant impact on an intractable social problem, have broad support and that can be replicated.

  Examples: the Ford Foundation, the Bill and Melinda Gates Foundation, and the Kellogg Foundation

- Regional in scope: some foundations, especially corporate foundations, are regional in scope because of the founder's interests, the hometowns of foundation trustees, or the footprint of the corporation's business.

  Examples: Bob Evans, Wendy's, Kroger, Procter & Gamble, and the William and Dorothy O'Neill Foundation

- State level: some private and corporate foundations limit their interests to a particular state for the same reasons listed for the regional foundations. In addition, the state of Ohio, for example, has departments, agencies, and other quasi-governmental entities having opportunities that are limited to Ohio.

  Examples: Ohio Department of Developmental Disabilities and Tennessee Developmental Disabilities Council

- Local level: many private foundations are interested only in serving their local communities, and some businesses allow their local store/unit to give grants.

  Examples: all community foundations, including family foundations, Walmart, Target, and Home Depot. There are also local organizations that have funds to use in the community and that may have a less formal request process (e.g., local Kiwanis, Rotary, Lions, or Civitan Clubs [among many other examples]; fraternal orders like Elks, Moose, Masons, etc.; and local women's or men's groups, such as the United Methodist Women, Thrivant Financial for Lutherans [formerly Lutheran Brotherhood], or Knights of Columbus).

Finding Funders Worksheet

What major national businesses are present or have an influence in my geographic area? (Consider major employers and major retailers.)

What government departments or agencies does my organization have a relationship with?

What community foundations serve my geographic area?

What local civic, fraternal, or benevolent societies am I familiar with in my geographic area?

Grant Research Next Steps

1. Create a list of prospects from your brainstorm above.

2. Look at the websites of your prospects (or speak to a member in the case of local organizations) and gather all the necessary information for applying for funding.

   You need to know/gather:

   - Eligibility requirements
   - What their specific interests are (or if they have specific RFPs pending)
   - When their proposals are due
   - Whom to send the proposal to
   - The form(s) and all specific application requirements

3. Eliminate any prospects for which you are not eligible or that have no interest in your program/project based on their stated mission and/or those with which you have no relationship. *Do not send applications to these funders.*

4. For those that may be interested in your program but with which you have no relationship, begin building a relationship by reaching out to the appropriate person and asking for a meeting.

To Recap

- Your fundraising activities should include as many of the commonly utilized vehicles for giving as possible:
  - Annual giving
  - Special events
  - Major or special giving
  - Planned giving
  - Corporate/foundation relations
- By putting your efforts into multiple vehicles, you will diversify your funding streams.
- Diversifying your funding streams not only provides a variety of avenues for donors to give but also strengthens their relationships with your organization.

Chapter Five

Building Block Four: Communications and Community Relations

IN THIS CHAPTER

- Learn how to tell your story
- Identify your audience of potential donors and key constituents
- Develop a plan for communicating with donors

One of the most fundamental requirements for success in fundraising is communicating your message and your story to the general public. The simple fact is that people give to organizations they are familiar with and that have a good reputation in the community. The way you go about making sure that people know who you are and what you do is through your communications and community relations.

Communications refers to your publications, such as a newsletter or magazine, your website, e-blasts, annual report, and even your event invitations. Community relations refers to your efforts to be visible in the community by participating in community events, advertising in local publications, sponsoring local events, hosting an event for the community, speaking engagements you may have with local civic or religious organizations, and to some degree your relations with local media (also called media relations). Organizations that have a full-time development or marketing staff person can keep up with these important tasks on a regular basis. But if you are the default fundraiser/marketer and you wear other hats too, you may find these tasks difficult and time consuming.

My suggestion is that, first and foremost, you craft your story.

Telling Your Story

When I first began working at St. Vincent Family Centers in Columbus, Ohio, I had a big learning curve when it came to understanding the programs and services offered by a pediatric behavioral health center and how they made an impact in the community. I asked a lot of questions and found that the answers were far too complex for most laypeople to understand. I sought a way of making the story gel so that it could be shared and articulated by our board, volunteers, and staff. Once I did that, my job as a fundraiser became much easier.

Here are some tips on how to get started on crafting and articulating your story:

- Interview staff. Ask your program directors or line staff what they do on a daily basis, why they think it is significant, and the changes they've seen since with clients. This will become the essence of your story.
- Understand the context. The work you perform in your organization is not done in a vacuum. There are many forces at work that affect you, positively or negatively. Knowing what those forces are and how they affect you is a key part of your story that others will want to know before they choose to invest in you. Seek out the people in your organization who can help you understand the bigger picture.
- Keep it simple. I've found in my career that when complex concepts can be articulated in just a few words, these words become powerful and the keys to effective storytelling. Try telling the story of your organization through a few key words or concepts.
- Put a face on it. Once you've gathered what you need to tell your story, put a face on your organization by sharing the personal testimony or a composite testimony of someone who has benefited from your organization.
- Give them the words. Your board and volunteers want to be able to articulate your story but sometimes feel awkward doing so. Literally give them the words to say by providing small pocket cards with talking points or by taking the time in a board meeting to allow them to practice with one another. The more opportunities they have to share your story aloud, the greater their comfort level and the more they will begin to share.

How to Interview Social Service Program Staff

One of the best ways to interview staff, especially in social service programs, is to ask them to elaborate on the reason for their program. Ask questions like: "What's happening to the people you serve before they get here?" or "If your program didn't exist, what would happen to the people who are being served?"

Continue with probing questions, and be sure to try to understand the larger context of what the program accomplishes by asking about how it fits into the system of services that serve that particular population. You can also ask what their biggest stumbling blocks are for accomplishing their work, and be sure to ask how they measure success.

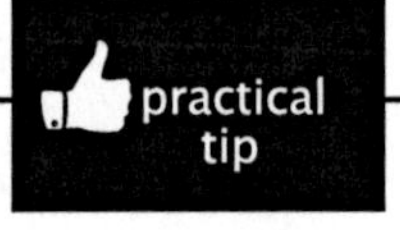

- Finally, keep it fresh by annually updating your story and any testimonies. These will form the basis of grant requests, marketing materials, speech copy, web copy, and even board orientation. So know your story, and then get out there and tell it!

Communication Vehicles

Secondly, consider what communication vehicles you can easily create and maintain that fit in your budget. A website is imperative in this day and age, but it must be kept fresh with new postings and ideally should be linked to a social media site like an organizational Facebook page. A weekly Facebook posting is sufficient, and two to three per week is ideal. E-blasts are also relatively easy to do, but they must be done regularly to be effective. Finally, an annual report is an excellent tool for building relationships with donors, including foundations. Many printers have in-house designers that can help you lay out an annual report without a huge expense. You might also consider creating one online only.

Common Communication Vehicles

Type	Frequency
Website	Update monthly or more frequently and completely revamp every three to five years.
Social media, including Facebook or Twitter	Post on Facebook at least weekly and Twitter one to two times daily.
E-newsletters or "e-blasts"	Disseminate one to two times per month depending on length and format.
Annual report	Disseminate yearly.
Printed newsletter	Disseminate monthly or quarterly.
Agency brochure	Update every two to three years depending on the amount of change going on in your organization.

Communication Plan

Finally, consider what audiences you want to reach, and be sure you are using the best vehicles for reaching them. Have a plan for what you want to accomplish by reaching each audience. For instance, if your goal is to increase revenue, then you must identify who needs to know more about your organization, develop a plan for communicating with them on a regular basis, and then assess if revenue increased through your efforts. Contracting with a consultant to help you develop these plans may make the most sense if you do not have this skill set or don't have sufficient time to devote to it.

For a thorough explanation of communication plans and how to design one, see the article by the Kellogg Foundation at fundraising123.org/article/developing-strategic-communications-plan.

Overall, addressing your communication with the community will make a lasting impact on your organization by building its reputation and increasing name recognition among potential donors and supporters, leading to increased community support for your organization.

To make a communication plan, start by completing the following statements.

Worksheet: Communication Plan

Our primary objective is to (e.g., increase name recognition):

Our secondary objective is to (e.g., increase media exposure):

Our key messages are:

Message one (e.g., our organization is making a difference in our community):

Message two (e.g., our organization is worthy of your trust):

Message three (e.g., our organization is worthy of your investment of time and resources):

___

___

___

In the table below, determine your specific audiences, which message they should receive, and what vehicle you will use to send that message. Then determine when and how often these messages will be sent, and be sure to include this information in your master calendar of fundraising/communications activities.

Audience	Message(s)	Vehicle	Timetable
Board/former board			
Specific donor set one			
Specific donor set two			
Specific donor set three			
Volunteers			
Staff			
Community leaders			
Prospective donors			
Other			

To Recap

- Donors give to organizations they know and that have good reputations in the community.
- The way to build a good reputation is by telling your story.
- Crafting your organization's story is worth spending time to do well.
- Consider what communication vehicles are the most useful and cost effective.
- Create a communication plan and assess the results.

Chapter Six

The CEO as Chief Fundraiser

IN THIS CHAPTER

- Learn why your development director wants to quit
- Discover the five steps to a successful relationship with your development director
- Embrace your role as chief fundraiser

As the CEO of your organization, you are tasked with many things, from operations to quality improvement. Fundraising is only one of your concerns. But did you know that everything you do affects fundraising? In fact, the most important factor in fundraising success is not the competence of your fundraiser or consultant but your own leadership and that of your board.

Keys to a Successful Relationship with Your Development Director

A survey done in 2012 by the Evelyn & Walter Haas Jr. Fund and conducted by CompassPoint Nonprofit Services found that one in four executive directors were so unhappy with their development directors that the last person to hold the job was fired, and more than half said they couldn't find qualified people to fill the role.

The interesting part of the study was that development directors felt the same way! A jaw-dropping 50 percent planned to leave their job in the next year, and 40 percent wanted to leave fundraising entirely. While there are many possible reasons this situation is occurring across the country, I believe, as the warden says in *Cool Hand Luke*, "what we've got here is failure to communicate." Many times boards, CEOs, and fundraising staff have different ideas about what the goals of fundraising should be. As we discussed previously, long-term success in fundraising is reliant on strong relationships, which take time to cultivate. Unfortunately, board members and CEOs often want immediate results that will impact their budget shortfalls right away. To meet the demand, fundraisers wind up taking shortcuts to raise big dollars, which leads to burnout.

I believe that if the goals were set differently in the first place, and if organizations understood some of the principles discussed in this book, folks on both sides would be a lot less frustrated.

Here are five key things your fundraiser needs from you as a leader in order to be successful, along with some tips if you aren't sure how to accomplish the suggested tasks. If you as the CEO are the default fundraiser, the following applies to you anyway.

Board Accountability

I can't tell you how many boards I've worked with or known about that did not understand their basic duties as members. As stated earlier, a board that does not embrace its fundraising role will not be successful in fundraising. I cannot emphasize enough that the board must understand its primary role, which is making connections in the community for your organization. This is one of the biggest hurdles that organizations face, especially small and medium-sized organizations.

If you find yourself faced with a board that does not understand its role and you aren't sure how to fix it, here's what to do:

- Complete a board matrix. There are templates online, or go to boardsource.org to find one. It's important that you have the right combination of talent and people of means on your board. If you have members who mean well but don't have connections, try expanding the number of allowed board seats by changing your bylaws, then begin bringing in the kinds of members you'd like to have. In this way, you'll begin to change the board's culture and makeup by degrees because doing it all at once is usually not possible.

- Find a fundraising champion on the board. Board members respond best to peer pressure. Make sure there is someone on the board who is motivating others to give and is staying involved in fundraising efforts. This could be the board chair, the development committee chair, a person of influence on the board, or someone with a real passion for fundraising.

- Conduct board training. If your board thinks it's not responsible for fundraising, hire outside counsel to conduct board training and help board members understand why it's critical to fundraise and how they can do it. The most effective board trainings help your members feel empowered, not forced. Finally, you do not need to spend a great deal of money on such training. It can be done very cost effectively and tailored to the needs of your board by finding an independent consultant in your area.

CEO Civic Engagement

The second key to a successful relationship with your development director is to recognize the importance of CEO civic engagement. By this, I mean that the leader of any nonprofit organization must be visible and active in the community, either through civic clubs, mission-related boards and committees, houses of worship, political activities (as appropriate), or all of the above. The reason this is important is, as the CEO, you must be aware of those situations or opportunities that may have a positive or negative impact on your organization, both short and long term. In fact, failure to be active in the community will undoubtedly relegate your organization to obscurity. Secondly, as the CEO, you must be visible in the community in ways that help you foresee those things that may have an impact on your organization long term. For CEOs of younger organizations or small to medium-sized organizations, I realize that prioritizing activities outside the office is difficult if you are spending most of your time putting out fires inside the organization. So here's some simple advice for increasing your civic engagement:

- Join a club. If you need to become more involved or be seen more in the community, join Kiwanis, Rotary, Civitan, Lions, or some other civic organization where you can "see and be seen." Then make sure attendance each week is mandatory! The more you put into these clubs, the more you and your organization will get out of them.

- Make time for fundraising and "friend-raising." Be sure you have appointments each month with key decision makers in your community and/or current or prospective donors. Talk with your development director about who those people are and keep tabs on these folks regularly. You may even want to keep a "short list" of prospects as a ready reference and check regularly to ensure you are making one or more key appointments weekly.

The Tale of Annie Ant and G. Hopper

Once there was a nonprofit fundraiser and an executive director. (We'll call them Annie Ant and G. Hopper.) All year long, Annie Ant worked hard creating relationships with donors: writing to them, visiting them, sending emails and newsletters. Everywhere she went, people knew her organization because of her efforts.

G. Hopper didn't think he needed to visit donors or be active in the community. Better to leave that to the "professionals" so he could focus on things like hiring and firing, and going to board meetings.

Soon difficult days came: there was a crisis that cast doubt on the organization's trustworthiness. Because the donors didn't know or trust G. Hopper, they began to fall away and donor support dropped. G. Hopper soon found he didn't have the personal community support needed to get through the crisis, and his organization began to falter.

It is wise to worry about tomorrow's sustainability today.

The most important thing is to prioritize these tasks on a weekly basis. Don't make appointments during your scheduled club meeting time. Force yourself, if necessary, to make at least one appointment each week that will generate support for your organization or cultivate a key relationship. If you have administrative help, enlist that staff member's assistance with helping you stick to your commitments. You and your organization will both reap the benefits.

An Organic Strategic Plan

The third key to success is an organic strategic plan. Your organization must know who it is, what its defining purpose is, and what it "wants to be when it grows up." Without this, everyone is lost, including your fundraiser.

By organic, I mean that your strategic plan should be a living document, used frequently as a tool for planning, and updated or reflected upon regularly. In other words, don't go through the process of strategic planning only to come out with a static summary of your organization's main goals. Your plan should reflect the vision you have for your organization, and it should have measurable action steps embedded in the document so that you, your board, and your staff have a road map for actually achieving the goals.

But what does your strategic plan have to do with fundraising? You and/or the chief fundraiser in your organization need to know what the priorities of the organization are in order to raise funds effectively. The strategic plan provides that guidance. Using the strategic plan, your development director can craft a fundraising plan that works in concert with the organization's vision for program expansion, new programs, capital needs, or other capacity-building activities. Without the strategic plan, the development director is "flying blind" and only guessing at what activities, programs, or plans need to be funded most.

So when it comes to your strategic plan, start by considering these questions: Do you have one? When was it created? Was it implemented? Does it still make sense? If you answered "no" to any of these questions, you need to make a strategic plan your priority for the current fiscal year.

A Comprehensive Fundraising Plan, Reviewed Annually

The fourth key to a successful relationship with your development director is formulating a comprehensive fundraising plan, reviewed annually. First, let me define some terms. I use the term comprehensive development program to describe the annual giving, major giving, corporate and foundation relations, and planned giving functions being undertaken by a nonprofit organization. I use the term fundraising plan to define the specific vehicles that will be used to implement your development program and how much each vehicle will raise. A development program may not change much from year to year, but a fundraising plan should be developed annually during your budgeting timeframe.

Although you may have hired a development director to create the fundraising plan, you cannot leave this person to implement it alone. You are the chief fundraiser and should be kept abreast of the fundraising plans and the outcomes your fundraising program is achieving.

Here's what to do:

Your job as the executive director or CEO is to work with your fundraiser to ensure that the comprehensive development program is working and has the resources it needs to be successful. Work with your fundraiser to create an annual *and* a three- to five-year plan for raising the money needed. The plan must state for what specific purposes the money will be raised and by what specific means. This is not the same as giving your fundraiser the budget gap for the organization and asking this person to fill it! Instead the fundraising plan becomes your road map for you both to track progress and constantly assess where you are going in case the landscape changes. And because change is inevitable, this plan cannot be reused year after year but updated and altered to fit the changing needs of your organization.

You can either make a fundraising plan or "buy" one by hiring outside counsel to help your chief fundraiser create one.

Become the Number-One Cheerleader for Fundraising to Your Staff

The fifth key to success is to become the number-one cheerleader for fundraising to your staff. Your fundraiser needs you to champion the cause to anyone who will listen, including your staff. Organizations that are successful in fundraising have CFOs, COOs, and main program people who are engaged in the fundraising process, and they have line staff that understands what fundraising is and how it affects them on a daily basis.

If you are in an organization that primarily looks to the development staff to raise funds, then there are times when the development staff may feel they are toiling in anonymity. You wear many hats as the CEO and engage many audiences on behalf of the organization, including your program staff and executive staff. So you may be the only means by which staff knows the efforts and successes of the development staff. When the development staff feel supported and see that you are taking pride in their accomplishments by sharing them with staff, they feel more motivated. And when staff see and hear about all that development is doing, they feel excited and want to participate. This leads to a broader culture of philanthropy in your organization, in which everyone sees the importance of their personal role in raising support for the mission.

If you're not sure how to achieve this in your organization, here are some suggestions:

- Be sure your chief fundraiser is given access to address your leadership team (managers, directors, etc.) and that this team is made aware of what is happening in development.

- Be sure to laud the successes of your development department in staff meetings, newsletters, and the like.

- Ask staff for their ideas about fundraising and empower them to take action on behalf of the organization.

Never Apologize

The most important thing you can do as the chief fundraiser for your organization is clearly articulate your mission and story to the community and ask for their support, unapologetically. There's nothing worse for a development director than to be in a public setting and hear the CEO say, "I hate to mention this, but..."!

You have the reins of your organization because you believe in the cause. You want donors and funders to be attracted to that cause. So when you are representing the organization in the community, never apologize for asking for support. Remember, your organization doesn't have needs; it has solutions to community problems. These solutions are ones that you should believe in so passionately that you want to share them with everyone you meet and ask them to participate. The conduit to this participation is you and your visionary leadership.

To summarize, your development director can make miracles happen, but without the support of you, the CEO, it isn't likely to occur. Work together to achieve the goals you have for the organization. You can start by knowing the invaluable role you play in fundraising success.

To Recap

- The CEO is the chief fundraiser of any organization and must understand the role as such.
- There are several practices of CEOs that make fundraising more successful, and utilizing these improves fundraising outcomes.
- Take the steps necessary to ensure you are benefitting, and not blocking, fundraising success.

Chapter Seven

What to Do If It's Just You: Managing the One-Person Shop

IN THIS CHAPTER

- ---➔ Determine your ability to handle this challenging job
- ---➔ Get focused on the two most important aspects of the job
- ---➔ Learn how to organize yourself for efficiency

There are many organizations that have no fundraising staff, are one-person shops, or have the CEO as the default fundraiser. Much of the information in this book is designed for these individuals, so definitely review the previous chapters for additional advice. For those who just need a quick guide to getting started as a one-person shop, this chapter will provide that.

The Importance of Passion

Recently I went out of town with my husband. We chose a getaway that would allow me to see and experience a bit of his new passion: white-water kayaking. After seeing the incredible amount of preparation, packing, traveling, unpacking, etc. (not to mention risk taking), he went through to participate in his new hobby, I exclaimed that the only way he could want to continue was if he was extremely passionate about the sport! The same is true for fundraising professionals who run one-person shops. Passion is a key attribute of any fundraiser, but especially those who are running one-person shops. In fact, passion may be the only thing keeping you going! So how do you keep your passion when you're toiling alone?

Reconnect with the Source

Take time in your day-to-day work to interact with those you are benefitting. Nothing will reconnect you better than seeing the faces of little children enjoying school, families receiving a meal, or patrons enjoying the artwork.

Plug in to a Community

Find others like yourself by joining AFP or another professional group and prioritize attendance. Learning new things about fundraising and sharing your struggles with others will make your situation seem so much more manageable when you feel like you're not alone.

Never Stop Dreaming of What Could Be

For years I kept a little paragraph on my bulletin board with this heading, and it always inspired me. Although I don't recall the source, this great sage reminds us that as fundraisers we are "dream brokers", allowing others to recognize all they could accomplish if their efforts were focused in the right place. The author encourages us to dream the impossible dream for our organizations and then share our dream with others in order to make it happen. Good advice, indeed.

> Although passion is the most important characteristic of a fundraiser, this is especially true if you have other staff to help you. Realistically, however, if it is just you doing everything, then please heed this advice: if you are not a highly organized, highly efficient person with great time-management skills, then this is not the job for you. Stop now. You will burn out quickly and become overwhelmed. Even if you are extremely passionate, please hand over the job to someone who is all of those things, even if that person is a consultant.

Getting Started Quickly

Even if you aren't the ideal person for this job (please see sidebar), I know you can't quit because it's just you and you need the job! So what should you do? Concentrate on two things:

- Your board
- Your donor communications

In essence, you will need to make your board your de facto development staff. Start by making sure there is a functioning development committee on the board. This group will be able to help you make key decisions and set short- and long-term goals; it can also run interference with the rest of the board to help your initiatives take hold. Managing this group will not be easy, but hopefully you can hand-pick the members and build individual relationships that will help you get the support you need.

The second step is to ensure that all fundraising projects have their own committees, including your annual fund. The committees do not have to be composed entirely of board members. In fact, it's a great way to recruit potential board members by introducing them to your organization on an event- or project-based committee. Then your job becomes managing the people on these committees and empowering them to undertake all the main fundraising projects of your year. Ideally, work with each special event committee beginning a year in advance of the event and help in whatever ways the committee needs, but do not do all the work yourself! Empower committee members to do as many aspects of the work as possible.

Setting Up Shop: The Basic Ten-Step Method

1. Identify your current donors and current corporate or foundation funders and gather as much information as you have on them in one place, such as a spreadsheet or database. You'll need the name of a key contact, address, phone, email, and any information on gifts they've made in the past.

2. Now analyze this information and determine who is giving what, through what methods, and for what purposes. Assign codes to various groups based on this analysis. For example, if a set of donors all gave supplies to a classroom, create a code for that type of giving. If another group gave through a mail appeal every year, create a code for "mail appeal" and add the date they gave. In this way, you can manipulate the data and pull out info on only the donors you want to target for a specific purpose.

3. Create an annual calendar of fundraising and communications/community relations opportunities. Plan for each of the following types of activities:

   - Mail solicitations
   - An annual fundraising event
   - An annual friend-raising event (such as a donor- or volunteer-recognition event or community event)
   - Grant proposals to foundations and/or corporations
   - A board-driven campaign/event/effort
   - Personal visits with your biggest or most devoted donors
   - Donor-appreciation efforts
   - A regular communication vehicle, such as a newsletter or e-blasts.

   Start small, keep your goals SMART (*S*pecific, *M*easurable, *A*chievable, *R*elevant, and *T*imely), and involve any key decision makers as you create the calendar.

4. Make a budget. Determine how much it will cost to do the activities on your calendar and determine a modest dollar goal for each effort. Be realistic about your goals so that you don't set yourself up to fail. Again, get the buy-in and approval of key decision makers in your organization, such as your CEO, key board members, or volunteers.

5. Using the calendar, create a detailed action plan for how you, your CEO, your board, and your volunteers can make this happen. Include timelines and specific assignments.

6. Work the plan. Don't forget to give regular updates to key decision makers about how you are progressing or any roadblocks you have encountered. It's better to tell them before or when it happens than have to explain it when it's too late.

7. Assess how things went, conduct a cost-benefit analysis of each effort, and decide what you would do differently next time.

8. Consider how you can attract new donors and research any other corporate or foundation donors you should be tapping.

9. Rework the plan based on the results of steps seven and eight.

10. Update your database.

Repeat!

This can be tricky because many committees believe it's their job is to tell you how to do yours! But with the help of a champion on each committee—by giving the members specific tasks and deadlines, managing them through reminder phone calls, and holding them accountable for their assignments—they should rise to meet the expectations you have set. Sometimes it will seem like it would be easier to do the work yourself, but it will be worthwhile in the end when the group takes ownership of the project and you see your base of support grow.

Second, as the manager of a one-person shop, you will need to make sure that your thank-you letters go out, that your data is clean, that you know your donors, and that you keep in touch with them on a regular basis through phone calls, letters, and other communications. This is by far the best use of your own time beyond managing the board and the committees. Failing to keep up with these tasks will inevitably lead to lost donations. Part of your job is making it look like everything is calm on the surface, even if you are paddling furiously under the water! Here's how to tackle this challenging feat:

- Set aside time each week to accomplish these activities. Find time in your week or, better yet, a few minutes each day to work on some of the "scut work" of correspondence, filing, and database entry. Don't let these things pile up or they will become overwhelming.

- Invest in a good database. The last thing you need as a one-person shop manager is to wade through volumes of spreadsheets and lists trying to find donor information. Instead, make the investment in a good, low-cost, web-based database system. You don't need anything fancy, but you do need something that has built-in capabilities to collect the information you need, to sort and manage that information, and to provide relevant reports.

- Hire a good assistant. I realize you might not be able to hire someone, but find a part-time person if you can. If not, you may be able to find willing volunteers on your board or through your local senior center, place of worship, high school, or college. Get creative and get the help you need.

- Find a reliable printer with a good in-house designer and do as many of your publications online or electronically as possible. I can't tell you how much time and money I have saved by finding a printer that is located in a small town (their prices are far less than the printers in my city) that has a good, capable in-house designer. This vendor provides high-quality work and is like having a "virtual" graphics department. I've also learned to do my own e-newsletters and other simple publications like postcards and flyers using desktop publishing and online resources. It's worth your sanity and your budget to seek out a good printer and learn these programs yourself.

One last bit of advice: throughout this book, I have written a lot about plans and calendars and lists. These will be essential for you as the one-person shop. But the most important of all of these is the master calendar. This one thing will be your saving grace if you make it and use it.

Here is how to make the master calendar: at the beginning of your fiscal year, put together a monthly to-do list of all the things that must be done that month to keep everything moving. It should include all the parts of your development operation (even if the tasks are all assigned to you!) and should be "backward planned" so that if an event occurs in a particular month, then everything that needs to be done for it is delineated in previous months. Similarly, if you want a newsletter to be received by donors in a particular month, then plan for collecting the info, writing it, designing it, getting it to the printer, and mailing it a month before you want it in the readers' hands. All these things go on the master calendar.

Month	Fundraising Mail, Events, or Other Campaigns Scheduled	Grant Proposals Due	Communication Vehicles This Month	Community Relations Opportunities	Personal Donor Visits to Be Made
January					
February					
March					
April					
May					
June					
July					
August					
September					
October					
November					
December					

Finally, use this book as a guide, create weekly to-do lists based on the master calendar, assess your annual development plans monthly, and review your strategic plans quarterly.

To Recap

- It's possible to be a one-person shop, but staying organized is key.
- Focus on your board and your donor communication.
- Make a master calendar and use it to keep yourself organized and on track.

Chapter Eight

Avoiding Common Pitfalls in Your Fundraising Career

IN THIS CHAPTER

- Learn to identify common pitfalls of fundraising professionals
- Gain valuable tips for avoiding burnout
- Stop and think before firing your development director or quitting your job

Fundraising professionals will tell you that they have the best job in the world and the worst job in the world. It's wonderful because they get to change the world with the work they are doing and they get to match the passion of donors with the world-changing missions of their organizations. It's also the worst job because it is easy to become overwhelmed, you often have competing priorities for your time and attention, and the need is usually very great and the resources very small. So as you begin a fundraising career, whether as an executive director, a development director, a board chair, or a volunteer, consider these potential pitfalls and plan ahead to avoid them.

Pitfall One: Underestimating the Importance of Volunteers

Fundraising simply can't be done without volunteers. We need them as board members, as committee members, as office help. And, of course, our programs often rely on them to ensure our missions are met. So having a volunteer management program is an important aspect of any development operation. Unfortunately, effective management of your volunteers sometimes falls to the bottom of the priority list and becomes "catch as catch can." I think the easiest way to manage volunteers is simply to help them be successful. Here are some tips:

- Volunteers want to feel useful. If you want to get the most from your volunteers, be as flexible as possible and allow people to use their individual talents on behalf of your organization whenever possible. Having volunteer job descriptions is a good starting point, but let volunteers make the job their own because a volunteer who feels useful will continue to serve or will become a donor to your organization.

- Volunteers want to be managed. Send volunteers to do only those jobs that are well defined, that have sufficient resources for accomplishing, and that can be evaluated. It's no fun to volunteer for an organization only to find that no one knows you are coming, you don't have what you need, and you never hear back from the organization about whether it made a difference.

- Volunteers want to feel appreciated. Make sure you include volunteers in your appreciation events and send cards, emails, or Facebook posts thanking your volunteers for the big and small things they do.

- Volunteers want to have an impact. If you show your volunteers that what they are doing makes a difference for your organization's mission, you will have a supporter for life. After all, that's the biggest reason most people volunteer! So let them know in any creative way you can.

- Volunteers want to share in your success. This tip applies to fundraising campaigns specifically. If volunteers have been responsible for accomplishing a major goal, be sure that they are given the credit they deserve as well as any public accolades you can muster. After volunteers see that they can be successful at raising money, they will return to raise more!

> Volunteers come in all shapes and sizes, from high school students and college students to young professionals to busy career executives to wealthy people with too much time on their hands. I've worked with them all, and each group needs a slightly different managerial approach. I love working with college students, for instance, but I spend a lot of my time helping them learn time management, follow-through, and basic business etiquette. Society women are another group that must be managed with kid gloves. These upstanding ladies can be a huge asset to your fundraising events but can be demanding and treat you like "the help." I've found that a volunteer job description and clear expectations that are communicated regularly help manage this challenging but important group.
>
> **food for thought**

Pitfall Two: Never Leaving the Office

We know that "people give to people" and that face-to-face asks are the best way to solicit funds but, oh, the pressure! Let's face it, the reality is that when we wear so many hats as development directors and CEOs, making those calls to get the appointments is so daunting that it just keeps falling to the bottom of our to-do list. We put it off and put it off and wonder why we aren't raising money! So what can you do about this problem? Personally, I believe you must have three basic things in place to get out of the office.

The Calendar

We all have calendars, and some of us have several, but the kind I'm speaking of is a planning calendar. At the beginning of the fiscal year, map out your visit strategy. How many people can you realistically see face to face per month? Set a realistic and achievable goal, and take into consideration other things that may be happening in that month that could prevent you from achieving your goal, such as holidays, vacations, special events, or other meetings. Set a goal you can actually reach so that you are motivated by your successes. You should probably also consider what days of the week and times of day work best for you to have meetings and block those times out on your weekly calendar so they are free for donor appointments.

The List

You can't make appointments if you don't know whom to call. Your monthly list should be composed of those from your inner circle that you need to keep in contact with one to two times per year as well as a handful of new folks you need to reach out to that you've identified through research. Have this list handy (in other words, don't rely on your database manager to provide it each time) and keep it up to date, keeping records of your visits and when to schedule the next one.

The Appointment for the Appointment

Finally, you must set aside time to make the calls. The best days to call are Tuesday through Thursday, and the best times are between 8:00 and 9:00 a.m. when people first get to their offices and after 3:30 p.m. when they are likely back in their offices from meetings. Plan your day to take advantage of these key times. Have everything you need in front of you, including a script if necessary. Then stand up and smile! That's right, stand up as you make the call to keep up your energy, and smile as you speak. It will come through in your voice.

When we leave the office to visit a donor, sometimes that visit is nothing more than a courtesy. One of my favorite donors was an elderly widow whose family had a fund with a local foundation that benefitted my organization and who also gave an annual gift. I tried to visit with her at least once a year and found those visits to be such a delight: just sitting in her kitchen or living room drinking tea and talking about her family and what her gifts were accomplishing at our organization. She enriched my life, and I think I helped her feel connected to the good works that she and her husband found so meaningful. It was well worth the time to steward this donor regardless of whether she ever increased her giving, simply because it was the right thing to do.

Another great way to handle making appointments is to send an email saying that you'd like to meet with the person in the next two weeks then have an administrative assistant call to make the appointment. Many busy people prefer to wave you through their "gatekeeper," then have "your people call their people" to set the date. But if you don't have that luxury, letting the person know you will be calling is always good form.

Pitfall Three: Failing to Identify, Cultivate, Ask, and Thank

This rule is one that seems so simple, doesn't it? After all, identification, cultivation, solicitation, and appreciation are Fundraising 101. But how often do we neglect to actually do all four things for every constituency that we have? I would wager that especially for those of us with small shops, it's an ongoing challenge. We go from one event or project to the next but fail to step back and look at the big picture. Exactly who are our donors, what do we know about them, and what are we doing to increase their giving? If you are unsure of your answer to these questions or you haven't seen evidence lately that your development director knows the answers to these questions, you may want to review these tips.

Identification

We tend to go back to the same donors each year but may never stop to realize that we're doing nothing to create new donors. Be sure when you create your annual goals and plans that you have some method of identification built in, whether it's through special events, a special mailing, board contacts, or even a donor database prospect-mining initiative. Capture as much information as you can about these donors and then include them in your fundraising efforts.

> **The Widow's Mite in Modern Times**
>
> Sometimes we look to the wealthy and the moderately well-to-do for our primary support. But consider that the most wealthy people in our country actually give only 1 to 2 percent of their net worth to charity annually, whereas those with much less give a significantly greater percentage. In other words, it means more and even hurts more for someone with very little to give a large portion of what they have than for the donor with excess. Judeo-Christian teaching suggests these are the people who will "inherit the kingdom." The elderly donor who gives ten dollars to your organization each year because of a connection to your charity but doesn't have much to give deserves your time and attention as much as the wealthy donor with the fat pocketbook whose motivation for giving may be much less profound.
>
> **food for thought**

Cultivation

Asking the same group of people for money each year without attempting to create a deeper relationship with these donors is a recipe for diminishing returns. Again, when you create your annual goals and plans, determine a monthly or quarterly plan for how you are going to reach out to your donors individually and collectively to inform them of what is happening in your organization, highlight an event of interest to them, or implement any of the other myriad methods to engage them in a personal relationship with your organization.

Solicitation

You may think you've got everyone covered, but do you? Check to be sure that no donors slip through the cracks each year without being asked by some formal method. Is there a group that is being missed? Be sure you know how each group is being solicited.

Appreciation

This is the easiest and most rewarding part of the job! Yet some of us have fallen into the habit of not thanking certain groups of people who give too little to warrant a heartfelt thanks. Remember the story of "the widow's mite" (see "Food for Thought" sidebar on previous page) and acknowledge that for some people, a small gift represents a huge commitment. Every donor deserves to be warmly thanked.

Once you've assessed your needs in these areas and addressed them, you'll be well on your way to increased giving and, more importantly, more committed donors ready to make a bigger investment in your organization.

Pitfall Four: Lack of a Fundraising Education Plan

Most development professionals have a limited budget each year for fundraising education. While a small purse may leave you feeling like you don't have much to work with, there are ways you can leverage those dollars for your benefit and that of your organization at the same time.

While I may be a little biased, I think the best bang for your buck is a membership in the Association of Fundraising Professionals. Yes, $305 a year is a lot of money—believe me, I know, since I now have to pay it myself! But active participation in the chapter gives you as many as eleven seminars, twelve audio-conferences, and a chance to win scholarships to attend at least one and sometimes two major fundraising conferences per year, both locally and around the country. If you don't get the scholarships, you get reduced rates. You also get access to the free resources on the AFP website, including free downloadable guides. Now that $305 isn't sounding like so much, is it? Check it out at afpnet.org.

Another great resource is the Foundation Center. It has a variety of reasonably priced trainings, and members also have access to its extensive libraries and resources. Depending on your job and how much grantwriting you do, this is another good investment.

Finally, there are multiple online resources that provide education, resources, and connections to paid and free help. Just put "nonprofit fundraising" into your web browser, and you'll find numerous options. CharityChannel.com is an excellent place to start.

No matter your budget, the main thing to remember is not to let the year slip by without a plan for continuing education. Think about what your organization and you as a professional need to improve your game. Target your education plan on those needs and make a commitment to attend. Continuing education can recharge your battery and make you a better fundraiser and thereby strengthen your organization.

Pitfall Five: Getting Burned Out

All of us feel stressed with our jobs, especially those of us who have a lot of pressure to perform, little reward, and almost no break from one stressful project to the next. Most of us can cope at least until the next vacation! But people who are close to burnout are different. They are paralyzed and no longer care about what happens. They can't see any hope that their situation will change. And, worst of all for nonprofits, they've lost the fire for the mission that once spurred them on and their stagnation is harming the organization.

So what can you do to avoid burnout and the risk of your nonprofit losing effective leadership? Here are a few ideas:

Keep It Real

Make sure in your day-to-day work that you stop and interact with those you are benefitting. Nothing will make you feel better than getting in touch with the people your organization serves. Make sure you take the time to smell the roses.

An executive director of a small nonprofit organization I worked with decided to resign from her position. We had been working together for several months, putting together the plan she needed to keep the fundraising part of her job moving forward and growing. All she had to do was follow the plan, but every time we met, nothing had been accomplished. It was so frustrating to me! I should not have been surprised when she told me she planned to resign. Not being one to hide my true feelings, I remember her saying, "I can see you're really upset that I'm leaving." But in my mind, I was thinking, "I'm not upset; I'm disgusted!" Now I see that what she needed was compassion: this woman was dealing with a classic case of burnout. In her current state of mind, she could no more have implemented my plan than fly to the moon.

Share the Load

Even if your organization cannot afford more employees to help you, find a mentor within or outside your organization or a group of people in your field and share the load. Talk about what's happening; they may be able to provide insight, suggestions, or just a friendly ear ready to hear you and share your burdens for a little while.

Regroup

So often when we work from day to day, we fail to stop and look at the big picture. Organizationally, we need to stop and conduct strategic planning, but what about personally? When was the last time you thought about your career goals and whether you were achieving them? Is there a future for you where you are? Do you need more education to take the next step on your journey? What's your personal strategic plan?

And, Finally, Take Vacation Time!

Those days are there for a reason. Plan at the beginning of each year when you are going to get away (even if it's a "staycation"), then leave some days unplanned for a last-minute break or unexpected need. You and your organization will be better for it.

Pitfall Six: Hastily Firing Your Development Director or Quitting Your Fundraising Job

Back in **Chapter Six**, we talked about the importance of the CEO to fundraising success and mentioned a recent study that showed how unhappy executive directors and development directors were with one another. I listed the five keys to success for working with your development director. If you implement these, your working relationship with that person should be positive, but if you are still struggling and considering firing that individual, stop and make sure you have done the following first.

Clarify Your Roles

Have an honest and open discussion about goals, your board, and the roles you, your board, and your development director play in fundraising. Listen.

Broaden Your Goals

Set some goals around the number of new relationships your development director builds each year in addition to the new dollars raised.

Provide Encouragement

Give your development director support in front of the board.

Make the Difficult Decisions

Work to make sure your organization's programs are self-sustaining so that fundraising dollars can be used for new programs, program expansion, or capital/equipment needs. In other words, don't make the development director responsible for keeping the lights on.

> The relationship between the chief executive and the development director has to be one of trust and mutual respect. I have been blessed in my career to work for executives I respected and who, by and large, supported me and believed in me. I learned early on that coming to my boss with a mea culpa before something went wrong was far better than waiting until the damage was done. I also found that taking an interest in what was happening to my bosses in their executive roles and staying abreast of how their personal lives were affecting their work lives gave me greater patience when working with them and ultimately greater insight into their characters. This approach built the trust and friendship that made my job that much more rewarding.

If *you* are the burned out and fed up development director your executive director wants to fire, here's some advice before you quit your job.

Identify Some Common Ground

When you have that honest and open discussion with your CEO, explain that you understand that the organization needs fundraising dollars to achieve its mission and that it's your job to lead the charge. But also explain that everyone must work together to achieve those ends. There are lots of good resources out there to help you gather the ammunition you need to make this argument. (And if you've tried this already to no avail, then you may need someone else to say it for you. Find someone your CEO respects.)

Set Friend-Raising Goals

Set some goals around the number of new relationships you build each year in addition to the new dollars raised. Help your CEO see that these new relationships have value for the long term, not just the short term.

Ask for Support

Ask your CEO to give you the support you need in front of the board and staff. Let your executive director know that when others see that the executive director is confident in you, then they will be also.

Ask Some Tough Questions

While you may not have any say in how your programs are run, do what you can to help make sure your organization's programs are self-sustaining so that fundraising dollars can be used for new programs, program expansion, or capital/equipment needs. In other words, if you are responsible for keeping the lights on, the organization has some "right-sizing" to do.

To Recap

- Remember your only job with volunteers is to help them be successful.
- Make a plan for getting out of the office and stick to it.
- Recharge your battery with fundraising education and planned vacation time to avoid burnout.
- Strengthen your relationship with your executive director or development director through a shared vision of the future, realistic goal setting and budgeting, and open, honest, and ongoing communication.

Appendix A

Fundraising Readiness Assessment

For each statement below, rate the truth of this statement as it pertains to your organization on the following scale:

1 = Not at all true (this is not happening in our organization)

2 = Somewhat true (this is true to some degree/we are working on it)

3 = Very true (yes, we have this one covered)

Statement	Rating
My organization is fiscally sound (programs are self-sufficient/operating in the black).	
The organization has been fiscally sound for more than two years.	
The organization has a succinct mission statement and vision statement.	
The board members understand their role in fundraising.	
There is a board-level development committee.	
A high percentage of board members give annually.	
Board members also contribute in other ways (volunteer, open doors).	
Board members can accurately articulate the mission, vision, and major programs of the organization if asked.	
The president/CEO/executive director serves on boards/committees or participates in other volunteer duties as a representative of the agency.	
The organization's president/CEO/executive director has experience in fundraising.	
The president/CEO/executive director has had professional training in fundraising.	

Statement	Rating
The president/CEO/executive director plays an appropriate role in day-to-day fundraising operations.	
There is a staff person other than the president/CEO/executive director who is responsible for fundraising.	
There is a sufficient budget for development activities.	
Development staff feel supported by the CEO.	
There is unity of vision and clarity of goals between the development staff and the CEO.	
The chief development staff person feels reasonably compensated.	
The chief development staff person has sufficient experience and/or training in professional fundraising.	
Development staff spends as much or more of their time in the community versus in the office.	
The organization has a donor database.	
The data in the database is in good condition.	
There is a staff person dedicated to database management.	
There are policies and procedures in place, such as check processing, gift acceptance, and adherence to the Donor of Bill of Rights.	
The organization has an organizational case for support.	
The organization has identified its funding priorities and updates them yearly.	
The board and staff agree on the fundraising vehicles to be used to achieve the fundraising goals.	
There is a formalized fundraising plan projecting one to three years that utilizes the agreed-upon fundraising vehicles.	
The annual fundraising goal does not represent more than 30 percent of the organizational budget.	
The organization has regular communications with its donors through newsletters or other publications, email, social media, phone contact, or in person.	
The organization participates in community relations activities, such as fairs, festivals, event sponsorships, civic group speaking engagements, and other related activities, on a regular basis.	
The organization conducts its own community relations event (special event designed to reach out to the community or provide education/information to the community.)	
Total	

33 to 54 Points

Your organization needs to follow the advice found in this manual and work diligently to bring up your score within the next six months to a year before launching a fundraising program.

55 to 77 Points

Your organization is well on its way to being ready for fundraising. You have several of the key building blocks in place, and you are ready to make fundraising plans and goals. Focus on the areas of this book that pertain to the statements above for which you received the lowest score. Make the necessary improvements and then use the tool to assess your organization again in six to nine months.

78 to 99 Points

Your organization is ready for fundraising! You have the major building blocks in place, your board and leadership are supportive, and you have sufficient relationships with potential donors to launch your fundraising plans. If you assess your organization at this level before reading this manual, then use the manual as a guide for training board and staff about the building blocks of fundraising. Or, if you've achieved this level of readiness after using this manual, then continue to use it as a reference to make sure you stay on track once you've launched your fundraising program.

Appendix B

Resources for Fundraising Training

The Fund Raising School: The Center on Philanthropy at Indiana University (philanthropy.iupui.edu/thefundraisingschool)

The Fund Raising School describes itself as "the only international fundraising education program housed within a university. We combine cutting-edge practice with scientific research in developing our curriculum." Courses are offered in different cities and online.

Courses: Association of Fundraising Professionals (AFP) (afpnet.org/professional/content.cfm)

"Courses range from first-course overview to professional development diploma and CFRE review. Also contact your local AFP chapter for events in your area."

Training: Network for Good Learning Center (fundraising123.org/training)

"Free online training on nonprofit marketing and online fundraising, supported by Network for Good and its guest speakers. Download slides, handouts, audio, transcripts, and other materials from past online sessions."

The Foundation Center (foundationcenter.org)

Widely regarded as the best resource for grant proposal writing training and foundation research.

Index

R

S

T

U

V

W

If you enjoyed this book, you'll want to pick up the other books in the CharityChannel Press **In the Trenches™** series.

CharityChannel.com/bookstore

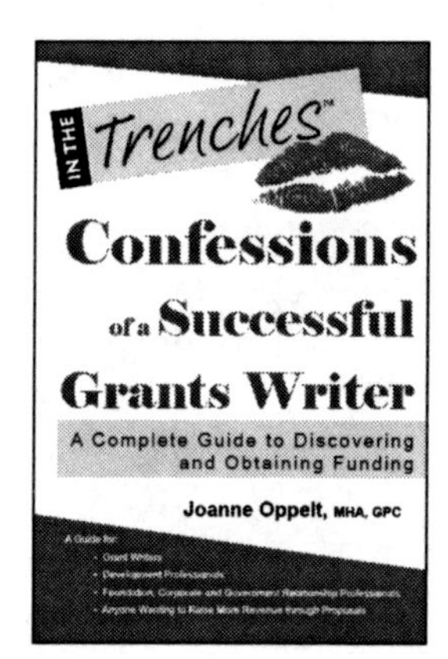

In addition, there are dozens of titles currently moving to publication.
So be sure to check the CharityChannel.com bookstore.

CharityChannel.com/bookstore

ForTheGENIUS.com/bookstore

Obamacare
for the GENIUS™
PLAN 1
PLAN 2
The Affordable Care Act and YOU!
Stacie Harting Marsh
FOR THE GENIUS IN ALL OF US™

CPSIA information can be obtained at www.ICGtesting.com
Printed in the USA
BVOW06s1811260814

364336BV00003B/5/P

9 781938 077470